Praise for *Thunder from a Clear Sky*

"*Thunder From a Clear Sky* tells an important and, until now, largely neglected story about the American Civil War. After sifting through a number of hard to find records, Ray Mulesky has produced an especially detailed and interesting account of how one particular border region of America suffered during the Civil War. Mulesky's book also reminds us how dark the days were for the Union cause, and how divided the border areas were during the first year or so of the conflict. *Thunder* stands as a fresh and important contribution in a field long studied."

—Professor Randy K. Mills, Ph.D., Oakland City University,
Author of *Jonathan Jennings: Indiana's First Governor*

Mulesky's account is deft, rendered in crisp prose.... History buffs will undoubtedly appreciate this illuminating account of an event outside the periphery of most history books.

—*Kirkus Discoveries*

"Well written...I found *Thunder From a Clear Sky* to be a fascinating read...I think anyone interested in Texas history would enjoy this book."

—John Hallowell, Publisher, *Texas Hill Country Magazine*

"His book is the most accurate that's been written about the raid."

—Michael L. Johnson,
Civil War authority

"The story of Adam Rankin Johnson's 1862 raid on Newburgh—the first Confederate invasion of the North during the Civil War—had not been fully told until Ray Mulesky took hold of it."

—*The Henderson Gleaner*

"An accurate historical account and an excellent read; a rare combination for a first-time author and one that makes me look forward to reading his future works!"

—*Southern Indiana Civil War Roundtable*

"Well written and well documented, this book provides a fascinating view of events of the raid on Newburgh."

—*Tri-State Genealogical Society Book Reviews*

"A fascinating account of how a skilled former Indian fighter gathered a few Kentucky rebels and "woke up" the slumbering Indiana Home Guard. Mulesky sees the humor in a motley contingent stealing an unguarded cache of weapons from a riverfront warehouse owned by one of Newburgh's leading citizens (without a shot being fired), but also focuses on divisions between neighbors in Civil War border states."

—*Evansville Courier & Press Book Reviews*

"A tremendous work. It brings this piece of history to life."

—Mike Whicker,
Author of *Invitation to Valhalla* and *Proper Suda*

The story of how one man, Adam Rankin Johnson, scoured the countryside near Henderson, looking for recruits for the Confederacy, and ended up heading up the group that was the first to invade the Northern state of Indiana. This is a MARVELOUS book and I highly recommend it to you.

—*Bluegrass Roots*
The Magazine of the Kentucky Genealogical Society

THUNDER

FROM A CLEAR SKY

THUNDER
FROM A CLEAR SKY

Stovepipe Johnson's
Confederate Raid on
Newburgh, Indiana

Written by
Raymond Mulesky, Jr.

iUniverse Star
New York   Lincoln   Shanghai

Thunder from a Clear Sky
Stovepipe Johnson's Confederate Raid on Newburgh, Indiana

iUniverse Star
an iUniverse, Inc. imprint

iUniverse books may be ordered through booksellers or by contacting:

iUniverse
2021 Pine Lake Road, Suite 100
Lincoln, NE 68512
www.iuniverse.com
1-800-Authors (1-800-288-4677)

ISBN-13: 978-1-58348-300-8 (pbk)
ISBN-13: 978-0-595-83623-9 (cloth)
ISBN-13: 978-0-595-83564-5 (ebk)
ISBN-10: 1-58348-300-4 (pbk)
ISBN-10: 0-595-83623-2 (cloth)
ISBN-10: 0-595-83564-3 (ebk)

Printed in the United States of America

To the memory of my father

CONTENTS

List of Illustrations xi

Acknowledgments xiii

Author's Notes xvii

Introduction xix

BOOK I
Henderson, Kentucky

Chapter 1   *The Union Garrison of Henderson, Kentucky* 3

Chapter 2   *Core Characters* 9

Chapter 3   *Attack on the National Hotel* 13

Chapter 4   *Somber Business* 17

Chapter 5   *"Whenever I find you, I'll hang you."* 21

Chapter 6   *Independence Day* 24

Chapter 7   *The Battle of Browning Springs* 28

Chapter 8   *A Diplomatic Correspondence* 31

Chapter 9   *Nicklin's Dangerous Bunch* 35

Chapter 10   *The Magnetic Pull of John Hunt Morgan* 37

Chapter 11   *An Open City* 42

Chapter 12   *King for a Day* 44

BOOK II
Newburg, Indiana

Chapter 1   *A Shiloh Veteran Comes Home* 51

Chapter 2   *The Bethells of Newburg* 56

Chapter 3   *Deadly Conspiracy* 61

Chapter 4   *Stovepipe Johnson's Confederate Raid on Newburg, Indiana* 64

Chapter 5   *The Bird Has Flown* 75

Chapter 6   *The Ugly Face of an Angry Mob* 80

BOOK III
Evansville, Indiana

Chapter 1   *Governor Morton Takes Charge* 87

Chapter 2   *Anxious for a Fight* 92

Chapter 3   *Rumors of Rebels* 96

Chapter 4   *A Union in Kentucky* 98

Chapter 5   *Solitude in Slaughtersville* 102

Chapter 6   *Union Bethell's Revenge* 104

Chapter 7   *Rural Encounters* 107

Chapter 8   *Redemption Declared* 110

Chapter 9   *Foster's Command* 112

Epilogue 114

Appendix

Cast of Characters 119

Event Timeline 123

Conspiracy: Elliott Mefford, Andrew Mefford, and Hamp Carney 132

The Soldiers at Newburg on July 18, 1862 140

A Short Analysis of Sources 143

Echoes of '62 147

Abbreviations 149

Reference Notes 150

Bibliography 169

LIST OF ILLUSTRATIONS

Northwest Kentucky xxii
Atlas to Accompany the Official Records of the Union and Confederate Armies,
plate 150 (edited)

Henry Turner Dexter 24

General Jeremiah Tilford Boyle 37

Thomas Bethell's Home 58

D. J. Lake & Co. Map of Newburg, Indiana, 1880 (edited) 68

The Exchange Hotel Hospital at Newburg, Indiana 69

The "Frame House" 71

The "Old Sandstone Mansion" 74

The Evansville, Indiana, courthouse 76

Indiana Governor Oliver Perry Morton 87

Lt. Colonel John Watson Foster 112

ACKNOWLEDGMENTS

When I took the first few steps up to the second floor of the Newburgh, Indiana, Public Library in July of 2002, I had no inkling that I was about to start a journey that would consume nearly three years of my life. The purpose of my visit was to research the connection between the Newburgh raid and the legions of Union recruits that filled Indiana regiments in the summer of 1862. The more I learned about Stovepipe Johnson's Confederate raid on Newburgh, Indiana, the more I was convinced that it was a story worthy of telling.

I was blessed in this project. Throughout the Midwest, I found people who were eager to assist me with source materials and advice. Without the help of these willing hands, this book would not have been possible. Among those who gave generously was Frank Nally of the Henderson, Kentucky, Historical and Genealogical Society. Frank reviewed my work, provided me with source materials, and took me on a walking tour to the very spot where Adam Johnson's men attacked the Union barracks in Henderson—a sense of awe filled us as we stood in such a historical place. Frank then sent me in the direction of Max Soaper, who lives on the same family farm where Johnson hatched the plan to invade Indiana the night before the strike. Max kindly discussed the background of his renowned ancestor, Mr. William Soaper, and provided insights into the published history regarding the night of July 17, 1862.

I visited Madisonville, Kentucky, and found Harold Utley of the Hopkins County Historical Society. He showed me where the Battle of Browning Springs was fought. The Browning Springs Middle School now stands on the very hill where the late-night gun battle took place more than a century ago. We walked on the western slope up to the summit where Johnson's "band of six" came up during the blackness of July 5, 1862, and attacked the 9th Pennsylvania Cavalry. The rolling slope was a small family cemetery in those times and now, more than 140 years later, it

is a somewhat larger cemetery. Harold told me something almost offhand-
edly that I've kept in mind ever since. He said, "Once something is wrong
in print, it's likely wrong forever." At the time I laughed, but like much
country wisdom it came back to me, and I understood.

One of the first to help me assemble events in Newburgh was local
researcher Michael L. Johnson (no relation to Adam Johnson). Mike talked
to me for hours, patiently walking me through events in the old part of the
city, following in the footsteps of the Confederate raiders on July 18, 1862.
Mike then introduced me to Don Claspell, who supplied me with important family background information on Hamp Carney, a pivotal figure in
the Newburgh raid. Also instrumental in assembling this story was Warrick
County, Indiana, historian Kay Lant. Kay provided crucial written accounts
of people who were present in Newburgh at the time of the raid. She also
provided me with the military records of Captain John H. Darby, the court
records of Ira Duncan, and photographs of homes involved in the raid. Kay
acted as counsel to me regarding the quality of the work throughout.

I am indebted to Dr. Randy K. Mills of Oakland City University, Indiana.
He had long anticipated writing about the raid but instead graciously
reviewed my manuscript, provided additional sources for this work, and gave
me welcome comments and encouragement.

I also thank the staff of the Special Collections Room at Willard Library
in Evansville, Indiana. I spent more time behind a microfilm reader there
than anywhere else for this book. The Newburgh Public Library; the
Evansville–Vanderburgh Public Library System; the Henderson County
Public Library; the David L. Rice Library at the University of Southern
Indiana; the Bentley Historical Library at the University of Michigan; the
Bower–Suhrheinrich Library at the University of Evansville, Indiana; the
William Henry Smith Memorial Library at the Indiana Historical Society,
Indianapolis; and the Indiana State Archives in Indianapolis were also
important sources of information for which I give thanks.

Finally, my thanks go to several special helpmates in this project—my
editors Cynthia Long, Aasta Carver, Amy Mulesky, and Spencer Mulesky.
My heartfelt appreciation also goes to Don Johnson (again, no relation to
Adam Johnson), who prepared the original book cover design and helped

with the interior graphics. The quality of this work would be far less without the enthusiastic help of my family and friends. They gave me the support to continue on through every doubt.

Author's Notes

I feel compelled to provide the reader with a few pieces of information before embarking on this story. First, I must comment on a trivial but potentially confusing point regarding town's name. The present-day town of Newburgh, Indiana, officially received the "h" at the end of its name in 1928 in order to reduce the number of postal mishaps between Newberry, Indiana, and Newburg, Indiana. One can understand how even good cursive penmanship could create problems in nineteenth-century postal service between the two towns. Unfortunately, like so much in the story to come, even this point is not one of clear demarcation. Apparently, the citizens of nineteenth-century Newburg were not particularly conscientious about spelling the name of their hometown one way or the other. Nevertheless, when Adam Johnson launched his raid, the official name of the town was Newburg, not Newburgh. From here on, when referring to the modern-day town, I have used the current name—Newburgh. When referring to the town of the nineteenth century, with the exception of the book title, I have used Newburg to maintain the historical accuracy.

In this work, it has been my solemn intention to write a true account of the notorious events surrounding the Newburg raid. In attempting to stay faithful to this promise, I have been faced with a riddle as old as the ancient poet Homer. Is it the job of the historian to simply unfold the sources and let the reader align them into a meaningful whole? Or is it the job of the historian to apply his or her expertise toward aligning the sources into a readable whole? Without debating these two questions, let me say that I side with the latter. Although this book is extensively sourced, I have presented some things in this work that aid the reader in creating a mental picture of events and that allow the reader to stand inside the story as it is happening. These items are carefully considered and are discussed in the endnotes. These details breathe immeasurable life into the Newburg story and provide an attraction and involvement that writers everywhere hope for their readers. Beyond these types of plausible scene-setting minutiae, the reader can be satisfied that even the phases of the moon and the uncertainties of the weather have been carefully researched for the story.

In the end, however, I have found that there is no such thing as "the true" account of events from 142 years ago. Understanding human history is a process, not a product. Vital sources are either lacking or lost, records are unclear or contradictory, everything is subject to interpretation, and some elements of the raid have passed beyond discussion and sources and into the immutable realm of folklore and legend. To me, researching this story was like assembling a puzzle with many missing and double-sided pieces. I humbly offer the contents of this book as one step in the process toward greater understanding of this historic event.

Finally, I have been told that publishing any work to the public is like releasing a beloved pet bird from its cage. After careful nurturing, once it is out, the life it takes on is independent from its former owner, and where and how it is received thereafter is up to those receiving it. When I began my research into a local southern Indiana Civil War regiment and wanted to know why so many Hoosier men enlisted during the summer of 1862, the story of the Newburg raid came forward as a contributing factor. At that point, I had no idea that this Yankee boy would stumble upon a nearly untold story about a Rebel icon.

INTRODUCTION

Summer 1862. Amid the late-night laughter and drifting smoke of scattered orange campfires, a small Kentucky company of Confederate cavalry raiders celebrates a bloodless victory outside Henderson, Kentucky. Its leader, Adam Johnson, rank uncertain, is meeting with two Indiana citizens. The subject of their conversation is a conspiracy that will cost the two Hoosiers their lives in less than thirty-six hours. Before the evening is out, some thirty horsemen break camp and make their way north toward the Ohio River. At the hot, hazy noon hour of July 18, 1862, Johnson and his loose band of like-minded Kentuckians cross the Ohio River in a surprise lightning strike, capturing the thriving river-port community of Newburg, Indiana. The raid is so well executed that within thirty minutes of landfall eighty-five Union soldiers in two local army hospitals and the commander of the Indiana Legion (Home Guard) company become prisoners. Not a single shot is fired by either side. Johnson's prize? Enough muskets and pistols to outfit three companies of Kentucky Rebels.

Five hours later, a looted, despondent town can only watch as boatload upon boatload of stolen guns and goods float off to Kentucky. Meanwhile, a nearby city has been alerted to the invasion and mobilizes a thousand men in less than an hour to rescue the beleaguered victims. City Home Guardsmen, convalescent soldiers, and angry civilians pile aboard three local mail steamers in an effort to hunt down the marauders before they escape. Also on board the steamers are several field artillery pieces prepped and ready for action. It is all too late. That afternoon, Indiana Governor Oliver Morton gets a telegram that he secretly expects and dreads—Confederate troops have invaded Indiana.

Undaunted, within seventy-two hours Governor Morton unleashes an impromptu invasion force of more than one thousand Union soldiers and sailors toward Johnson's base of operations in Kentucky. The specific pur-

pose of their mission is to hunt down and destroy the emerging Rebel company and return stability to the Ohio Valley.

This is a different kind of Civil War story. In this story, the closest we
will get to Union General Ulysses S. Grant will be a brief mention of his
wife and children. The closest we will get to Confederate Lieutenant
Colonel Nathan Bedford Forrest will be a single, quick ride through his
camp. While the heralded names of Antietam, Gettysburg, and
Chickamauga occupy their justifiably distinguished positions in the
nation's Civil War history, there was another war underneath these great
milestones—a war no less real or deadly to the citizens and soldiers who
took part. This is the story of the Civil War as seen by the Kentucky countryside. During three weeks in the high summer of 1862, we witness the
drumbeat of Adam Johnson's campaign to draw forth a regiment of
Kentucky Confederates from a divided populace using no more than himself and his own enterprising deeds as recruiting tools. It is a story of surprise nocturnal strikes, opportunistic military occupations, and finally, a
bold daylight incursion into the Northern homeland. Like tumblers click-
ing in a combination lock, unrelated events combine to open the bustling
riverside community of Newburg to attack from an intrepid Kentucky
icon. This book is about the high watermark of partisan warfare, the first
Confederate military operation to cross north of the Mason-Dixon Line
during the Civil War. As reported in the *Daily Evansville Journal*, the raid
was like "thunder from a clear sky." It was a bold, unexpected stroke by a
bold, unexpected soldier.

Did the busy Indiana river town have any warning of an impending
attack? There was no warning of a specific attack on a specific day, but,
sadly for Newburg, there were warnings and unfulfilled intentions leading
up to the raid—any one of which could have changed or prevented the
deadly outcome. But Newburg didn't need a warning from outside the
town to stimulate concern; any unbiased assessment of Newburg's vulnera-
bilities would have quickly revealed its true security status. The town had
a seriously depleted and essentially inactive Home Guard. The large store
of idle weapons so near to the river was plainly a careless choice of place,

and the significant increase in Rebel activity in northwest Kentucky in early July was an ominous, unheeded forewarning. A population with a known mix of views on the war and slavery meant unrest was just under the surface in Newburg, and no one saw the unfettered approach from the river as anything other than a vehicle for commerce. It certainly cannot be said that southern Indiana had no way of knowing what would happen. Decisive action even minutes before the Confederate landing could have changed everything. But just because hindsight has offered a different path doesn't mean there is blame. Before every event in human history, choices exist for different outcomes.

Even now, as an event firmly in the past, what is the story of the Newburg raid? Is it one of courage and guile, or is it one of betrayal and revenge? Is Adam Johnson a petty thief and a murdering pirate, or is he a heroic underdog and a military genius? Is Union Bethell, the Newburg Home Guard captain, a negligent coward or an avenging angel? Or are the attributes for each man better placed with the other? From this point forward, the reader decides.

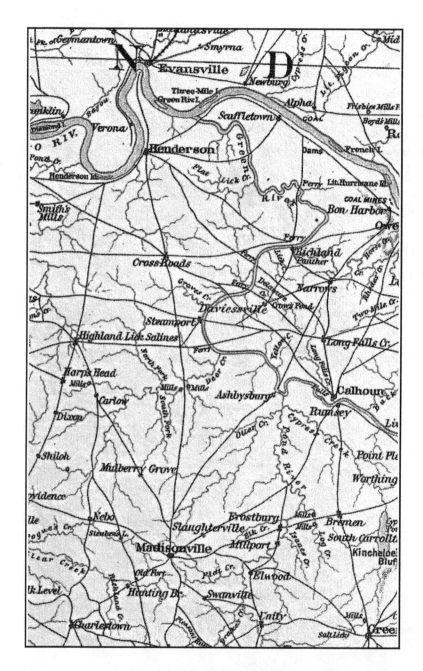

Northwest Kentucky
Reprinted from the *Atlas to Accompany the Official Records of
the Union and Confederate Armies*, plate 150 (edited)

"That an insignificant band of guerrillas could dare to invade free soil was a piece of temerity absolutely incredible. Yet that thing was done. Our people were startled as by a clap of thunder from a clear sky."

—*Daily Evansville Journal*, July 26, 1862

BOOK I

HENDERSON, KENTUCKY

CHAPTER 1

The Union Garrison of Henderson, Kentucky

AS THE SUN SLID DOWN on the Sunday afternoon of June 22, 1862, Senior Second Lieutenant George B. Tyler stepped off the steamer *John T. McCombs* and onto the creaking wood of the Henderson, Kentucky, wharf. He tried to take a deep breath, but it was no use. Charmingly characterized as "sultry" by the locals, it was the kind of hot, humid day that he and his Coldwater, Michigan, men weren't used to. His shirt was clinging to his back from sweat. With the exception of a quick stop at Owensboro to pick up orders, Tyler had spent much of the 170-mile float down the Ohio River from Fort Duffield quietly enduring the oppressive heat while absent-mindedly staring at the Kentucky shoreline. Unknown to Lieutenant Tyler on that hot summer Sunday, in a week's time he would once again be on the same steamer returning upstream from where he had come.[1]

Initially, the Henderson townsfolk had mistaken the faded scarlet pant stripe of their Union army uniforms for cavalry. These, however, were the men of the 1st Michigan Light Artillery Regiment, Battery F—known by the soldiers as Andrews's Battery in recognition of their commander, Captain John Sidney Andrews. They had quietly spent their first three months of field service on garrison duty at Fort Duffield in the peaceful river community of West Point, Kentucky, just southwest of Louisville. During the bloom of the mild Kentucky spring, the men had done easy time with virtually no enemy contact. Although many had fallen ill, there were as yet no combat casualties.[2]

Lieutenant Tyler's first glance up at the twilight-clad dwellings on Water Street left him with the initial impression that things could turn out to be comfortably similar to his last assignment upriver at Fort Duffield. After exploring for a few hours, he changed his opinion. In the early summer of 1862, Henderson was a town in turmoil. After the bloodiest battle of the war in early April, the Tennessee River had gushed forth a deluge of sick, wounded, and dead from the killing fields of Pittsburg Landing. These broken bodies were taken to every port of call down the Tennessee River and in both directions on the Ohio between Cairo, Illinois, and Cincinnati. Henderson was no exception; its hospitals were still filled with hundreds of wounded when the Michigan men arrived in late June. The hastily erected military hospitals in river towns throughout the Midwest became notorious breeding grounds for every type of infection. Pneumonia, typhoid fever, measles, dysentery, and smallpox shadowed the dingy gangs of debilitated humanity wherever they were taken. In Henderson, smallpox had just spread from the soldiers to the civilian population. People began to hide in their own homes. Add to this an increasingly bold run of recent local guerrilla activity, and it was a town with dangerous underlying currents.[3]

Of course, there was much about Henderson that couldn't be learned from a short tour. Hidden under the everyday summer bustle in the downtown area was the fact that Henderson, a town of barely four thousand people, had found a vital, almost unique economic niche. Some of the best tobacco in America was tended on farms ringing the town, and it was a product with steadily increasing demand. Per capita, Henderson was one of the richest places in the world. But the wealth of Henderson County was built on a devil's bargain; more than forty percent of the population was slaves. This was more than twice the percentage across Kentucky as a whole. Henderson, split on the subject of secession, was virtually unanimous on the subject of the president and his presumed outlook on emancipation. In the election of 1860, Kentucky native Abraham Lincoln got a total of five votes in Henderson County, less than one-half of one percent of the vote cast. In four of seven precincts, Lincoln did not get a single vote. Kentucky was one of three states that went to former Speaker of the House of Representatives, U.S. senator from Tennessee, and Constitutional Unionist candidate, John Bell. Politically, there could be few places further apart than Coldwater, Michigan, and Henderson, Kentucky. Most of the Michigan volunteers had never seen a slave before arriving in the South.[4]

The new military commandant of the Department of Kentucky was a forty-four-year-old Kentucky lawyer, educated at the College of New Jersey, named Jeremiah Tilford Boyle. Brigadier General Boyle had declared himself for the Union earlier than many in Kentucky and, although somewhat excitable and completely without military training, had conducted himself well as a brigade commander at the Battle of Shiloh. As a reward for his exemplary service and as a prominent Bluegrass Abolitionist, the rotund Boyle had been promoted to his new office with the hope that he could calmly secure the unstable border state for the North. He had barely ascended to his new Louisville headquarters when he made the decision to shuffle the fifty-man detachment from Andrews's Michigan Battery to Henderson.[5]

The Michigan soldiers were assigned to gather intelligence on the town's sympathies; to make an orderly, positive presence to the locals; and to arrest anyone engaged in activity that could benefit the enemy. Apart from soldiers on light duty in hospitals, they would be the only healthy, active Union army presence in town. Tyler soon received a briefing that led him to the unavoidable conclusion that "the country nearby...had been invaded by guerrilla bands." Two days before Andrews's Battery arrived in Henderson, the McLean County Courthouse at Calhoun, which was a day's ride to the southeast, had been sacked and firearms had been confiscated by a band of Confederate irregulars. On the same day as the Calhoun raid, Major John F. Kimbley, chief surgeon of the 11th Union Kentucky, had been bushwhacked just fifteen miles away on the Owensboro Road near Hebbardsville. After being interrogated, Kimbley was taken into the backwoods near Green River, summarily relieved of his $600, two-horse carriage, "paroled," and then dumped off in the midnight wilderness. He was eventually "picked up by a steamer and brought back to Louisville where he complained bitterly of the event to General Boyle." The enemy was active and near.[6]

On top of these concerns, Tyler had a serious prospect of trouble from within. First, Battery F was a well-trained, hard-drilled group of cannoneers, but they were sent to Henderson without any artillery. This was a prescription for boredom and all its ill effects. Second, no one knew much about guerrilla tactics, the primary means of enemy activity in the area. Finally, long months of uneventful duty deep behind the front lines had given Tyler's men a potentially unrealistic view of wartime Kentucky. It was a lot for a twenty-eight-year-old to think about.[7]

Commanding the detachment was Tyler's good friend and amiable mentor, forty-two-year-old First Lieutenant Luther F. Hale. Tyler was Hale's right-hand man, and while Hale was introducing himself to the mayor and others of importance, Tyler would be handling day-to-day activities with the men. After some preliminary scouting, Tyler made the most important decision of his young life; he decided to recommend the National Hotel, a stern-looking two-story brick building on North Main Street, as the detachment headquarters. It was positioned close to the waterfront near most of the action, and it was big enough to comfortably accommodate their numbers. Hale agreed with Tyler's choice, and the Michigan artillerists settled in as a grand, silver vein from a summer thunderstorm flashed down from the west over the river.[8]

For the two days following their arrival, the wary Michigan soldiers kept a low profile and made no arrests. The town seemed quiet enough, and the men in blue didn't have to look far for trouble. More than any external concern, the artillerymen bemoaned the lack of equipment. True to Tyler's anxieties, the lack of a proper battery combined with uncomfortable weather to foster an environment of boredom, sniping, and poor morale. Just as the men had begun to settle into an uneasy routine, Wednesday, June 25 "opened early with heavy rain and continued all day so dusky, dark and drizzly, murky, muddy and miserable that everyone's spirits went down to zero." Lieutenant Hale curtailed activities in recognition of the wet weather. With everyone jammed into the hotel to escape from the pelting rain, things once again got testy inside.[9]

Late that afternoon as the clouds split, allowing the sinking sun to spread an orange fan on the western horizon, Lieutenant Tyler received surprising news that the *Forest Queen* had just let off a company of Union soldiers dockside. General Boyle, unannounced to Battery F, had decided to bolster the Michigan contingent with a sixty-man detachment from the Provost Guard of Louisville, Company E.[10]

The Michigan officers quickly buttoned their tunics and hustled down to the landing. Captain John O. Daly received the salutes of Hale and Tyler, introduced his staff—including his younger brother Second Lieutenant Eugene O. Daly—and put everyone at ease. The soaked, tired guardsmen were led up the red, muddy bank to the National, where they took off their wet outer clothes and introduced themselves around. Daly's men were Kentucky boys who had been in the business of hunting down renegade secessionists and handling prisoners for almost a year. During that time it was not unusual for members of the guard to pull duty transporting prisoners up and down the Ohio River, either for exchange at Cairo or imprisonment in Louisville. Henderson was not a foreign destination for them. Even though no trouble with the Rebels had erupted yet, Tyler was glad to see the Louisville Guardsmen. Arriving late, Daly decided to bunk his men in with the Michigan unit. The entire Federal force of some 110 cramped soldiers was now all in one spot. It was the first in a series of missteps that would result in deadly consequences.[11]

The "muddy, misanthropic" deluge continued through the 26th, but the enterprising captain of the Louisville Guard was not deterred. Captain John Daly made it clear that things were going to be different in Henderson. It wasn't long before he made himself known, cranking up the information-gathering machinery and developing several leads on Confederate activities within his first forty-eight hours in town. By June 28, Daly had bagged a local named Garrett Mitchell and had him promptly sent off to Louisville; he was the first of many dubious suspects to make the long journey upstream in shackles to sit in Federal military prisons indefinitely. Whether the locals appreciated all this newfound attention was doubtful. Folks from Henderson, like every neutral party in the history of warfare, found themselves to be the uncomfortable beneficiaries of scorn from both sides. Even loyal Union townsmen were placed under a blanket of silent suspicion by the bluecoat patrols on the streets. For the Federal soldiers stationed in an overcrowded, disease-ridden, guerrilla-infested Southern river port, everyone was a potential threat. Hale wrote to Captain Andrews at West Point, "They go disguised not in uniform, but in citizen's dress bound together in small bands and commit their outrages on individuals and skedaddle." There was an element of fear everywhere.[12]

It didn't take long for word of the Union troop arrivals to reach the countryside. To those who believed in the Second War of American Independence, the existence of an occupying Lincolnite garrison in Henderson was a flagrant provocation. To Confederate soldiers actively engaged in the struggle for the future of Kentucky, the presence of the newly arrived Federals meant that the enemy had arrived and that it had to be opposed.

CHAPTER 2

Core Characters

Prowling the border of Henderson County was another twenty-eight-year-old man committed to cause and country; his cause was Southern independence, and his country was the Confederacy. He had been assigned to his home region to collect recruits and to take the war directly to those forces occupying a reluctant Kentucky, a state whose rightful place belonged with the other seceding entities south of the Ohio River, a state whose star was in the very middle of the crossed bars on the banner of a new nation. The man who turned out to be the prime mover of events in northwestern Kentucky during the summer of 1862 embodied a combination of characteristics that made him the subject of both heroic admiration and passionate contempt. His name was Adam Rankin Johnson, the original "Kentucky Swamp Fox."[13]

"Ad" Johnson grew up in the Henderson-area farm fields and back-woods of the Green River swamps during the 1840s and 1850s. To those who knew him from his earliest age, he was a natural-born leader. As a child, he was always inventing elaborate tricks at the center of his boyhood gang. He demonstrated a daring propensity to concoct and lead the type of adventures that would make him well-known as an extraordinary personality among his peers. Even as a young schoolboy, Ad Johnson constantly stretched his thinking to find the advantage in any game or gamble. To those who were victimized by the "plank spanning the puddle with its cracked side down," he was a troublemaker. To his boyhood band, he was a source of admiration as one who could cleverly manifest the mischievous underside of childhood.[14]

He was a young man of physical and mental fearlessness—a legendary expert with a gun, a fishing pole, a swimming hole, or any other endeavor he put his mind to. He counterbalanced the risk of physical danger with seemingly unlimited nerve. Though decisive and daring, he was never rash, according to his wartime nemesis and prewar childhood comrade, James Holloway. "As a leader among the boys, [he] got us into and out of many scrapes."[15]

When Johnson was twenty he left Henderson to make his fortune where the American frontier was still being hacked from raw nature—west Texas. While there, the skills kindled in childhood gave off a glow that attracted others. He spent the next eight years of his life bringing his distinctive brand of courage and chicanery to whatever tight spots presented themselves. He fought the tribes of the Comanche almost continuously during his time as an overland mail stage-coacher and surveyor, and when Texas seceded he found his sentiments shaded by his years in the South. By the time he returned to his hometown in early 1862, Adam Johnson was perhaps the most battle-seasoned man in the state, a veteran of many deadly confrontations of all manner and description. Out of frontier necessity, he became an expert in combat misdirection and illusion. Even though regularly outnumbered by his Texas plains opponents, he had come out whole on the opposite side with guile and luck. For better or worse, there were few people like Adam Rankin Johnson in Henderson County, Kentucky, then or since. He was a man of action, particularly equipped for the task at hand.

Adam Johnson first met his hero, Confederate General John Breckinridge, in May of 1862 near Corinth, Mississippi. By the time of the Civil War, John Breckinridge had crafted a career that put him in the top rank of American politicians. He had been vice president in the Buchanan administration, Democratic Party presidential candidate in 1860, U.S. senator, member of Congress, and Kentucky Democratic Party leader. When Adam Johnson was sixteen, he came into the employ of a wealthy Henderson tobacco dealer, David R. Burbank. Burbank and Breckinridge were close friends and entertained at each other's homes before the war. Burbank's association with Johnson brought the young Southern soldier to General Breckinridge's headquarters in May of 1862. Once there, Johnson received an encoded message to deliver to Burbank and obtained orders to form a Confederate regiment from western Kentucky.[16]

Johnson's mission was to assemble a Confederate cavalry regiment from a Kentucky countryside mixed in its proclivities—so mixed that the war had toppled the branches of his own family tree. Brothers Ben and Thomas, who had been with Adam in Texas all these years, enlisted in the Texas Light Artillery, 6th Field Battery. However, his parents in Henderson were well-known Union supporters, and brother William S. Johnson was a lieutenant in the 17th Union Kentucky Infantry. Such was the strangely typical plight of many Kentucky families during the war.[17]

When Adam Johnson started his mission, he didn't even have ink-on-paper orders; he had to do everything himself. Not only was he to accept recruits, but also he personally had to create the reasons for them to come forward. Once in hand, he had to find arms for them, and, once armed, he had to lead missions for them. To this difficulty was added the fact that his recruiting landscape was nominally under Federal control and that many weapons and horses and much equipment had been taken into Union service. The true dimensions of his task would prove daunting.

His grassroots effort to create something from nothing began slowly, too slowly for a man with such a short stretch of patience. Although many young men were sympathetic to his cause, Johnson's apparent youth and inexperience, along with the desire for men to remain near their hometowns, conspired to present a frustrating outlook. Through the early weeks of June 1862, Johnson and his sole companion, Bob Martin, carefully and quietly canvassed Webster, Daviess, and Henderson counties with disappointing results—not a single recruit between them.[18]

Johnson and the tall, lanky Martin were to become so close in their future exploits that they were nearly always mentioned in the same breath. When Johnson entered Confederate service in late 1861, he found himself in the Hopkinsville, Kentucky, camp of Lieutenant Colonel Nathan Bedford Forrest with a request to become a scout for Forrest's cavalry operations. After interviewing Johnson, the Confederate colonel introduced him to the soldier who would become his closest confidant during the war—Robert Maxwell Martin. Forrest's orders were for the two to work together. Their personalities clicked, and from that moment on they were inseparable.[19]

Sometime in the middle of June, while recruiting door-to-door, they found the first volunteer to Johnson's group—Francis Amplias Owen. Owen was a fair-haired, five-foot seven-inch boy who'd already experienced harsh service in the Confederate army. He had been "wounded and captured at the Confederate surrender of Fort Donelson in February 1862 and became a prisoner of war at Camp Morton, Indianapolis." He escaped in April and made his way south on foot, dodging close calls around each turn. The final part of his escape was made on a steamer full of Union soldiers crossing the Ohio River to Kentucky. By the time he joined Johnson in June 1862, the hard-boiled Owen had barely turned seventeen years old. These three men—Johnson, Martin, and Owen—were the core characters on the Confederate side of events in the summer of 1862.[20]

On June 20, the trio's luck changed when a major in the Union army practically fell into their hands while the three were calmly discussing matters on the roadside near Hebbardsville. After easily overhauling the unsuspecting carriage rider, Johnson seamlessly slipped into the artificial persona of Confederate commander "George Davidson" and loudly began invoking nonexistent squadrons within Major Kimbley's open earshot. The entire scene was skillfully formulated to impress Kimbley with the image of Confederate soldiers filling the Kentucky forests. It would be the first of many spontaneous, deceptive stage acts put on by Johnson designed to confound and mislead the opposition. This time it worked too well, however, resulting in a company of Louisville Provost Guard troops showing up in Henderson as a consequence. While in Slaughtersville and still contemplating his lack of success in drawing forth the faithful, Adam Johnson received news of the Louisville Guardsmen. It was Saturday, June 28, 1862.[21]

CHAPTER 3

Attack on the National Hotel

Sunday morning, Johnson began to map out an attack on the Union barracks at the National Hotel in Henderson. To the former Indian fighter, the mission was a straight military operation. The fate of Kentucky was in the balance, and the enemy had invaded. Johnson would reduce their numbers, stake a Confederate presence in the city, and marshal the necessary credibility to bring recruits in from hiding across the region.

Guerrilla operations depend upon superior intelligence and secret intent; Johnson had both to his advantage. He knew the area like the back of his hand, having worked at the Barrett factory across the street from the National Hotel as a teenager. No one in town said a word that day as Johnson quietly rode the neighborhood in the disguise of his normal rough-riding life. Despite a purposeful low profile, Johnson was too well-known to get very far in Henderson without being recognized. Hours before the attack, locals knew something was about to happen.[22]

On the quiet Sunday evening of June 29, as the sun slowly melted to a shimmer beyond the western Ohio River, the little stern-wheeler *John T. McCombs* eased onto the Evansville wharf and unloaded the wife and four children of General Ulysses S. Grant. The family had come down from Louisville for an overnight stop at the American House Hotel on their way to visit the general near Memphis. At that same moment, twelve miles due south, Johnson, Martin, and Owen checked their loaded shotguns, saddled up, and rode toward the National Hotel.[23]

With night now in control, the insurgents arrived at a secluded wood-lawn on the southeast part of town about a half-dozen blocks from the National. Three silent ghosts quietly tied their horses to the trees of Alves's

Grove and cautiously moved toward Fourth Street near the river. They turned right, gingerly walked up behind the Barrett Tobacco Stemmery, took their positions, and waited. The threesome calmly observed the choreography of the unfolding scene. It was a perfect setup. A sunken fence had been erected adjacent to the Barrett building, and a gaslight street lamp had been installed in front of the hotel. Johnson's men would be cloaked in darkness behind a fencerow, and their victims—unaware and defenseless—would be well lit on the pavement. Under the capsule of light held by the sidewalk lamp outside the National, about a dozen sweaty, exhausted soldiers were sprawled on the brick pavement, the murmur of conversation floating through the warm night air and the smoke of pipes drifting up in silhouette.[24]

It was a long, hot night. Lieutenant Tyler and the two Dalys had been out walking in front of the hotel when they decided to sit down on the steps leading into the hotel barroom. Just past midnight, the casual serenity of insect sounds in the still, hazy night was shattered by the volcanic boom and flare of six rapid shotgun blasts from the fencerow across the street. Soldiers collapsed onto the ground like lumber, and a mad, man-over-man scramble for the door ensued. The raiders pulled back behind several tall stacks of barrel staves and reloaded. They could hear the screams and confusion over the top of the fence as they calmly refilled their muzzleloaders.[25]

Lieutenant Tyler barreled through the door of the hotel yelling, "Oh, I'm shot. I'm shot!" Captain Daly, hit in three places, bellowed that the barracks were under attack and for all hands to rally. The dumbstruck Union soldiers scampered outside and pulled the moaning wounded through the hotel doorway. The lights were cut, and moments passed in chaotic disarray. Lieutenant Hale, abruptly roused from slumber by the sudden racket, shook off the cobwebs in time to theorize that the attack out front could be a diversion and lined a row of pickets outside off each of the rear wings of the building. Just as the pickets had crouched into position, they came under attack from the direction of the old Henderson Cemetery behind the hotel. A figure came bounding out of the darkness, pulling on a pistol trigger with one hand and holding a shotgun with the other. Battery F Private John Gould cried out and hastily limped back through the rear door, wounded. In rapid succession, four more lightning shotgun flashes licked out of the bushes toward the back door, felling several more guardsmen before the Federals returned fire.[26]

Inside the National, anarchy reigned. The men had been ordered to sleep on their arms, so all had either taken positions quickly or begun tending the wounded. Those who had been hit were soaking the floorboards red, and the entire house was alive with the frenzied clatter of footsteps and the cacophony of voices. Believing themselves surrounded, the Louisville Guardsmen were now returning fire into the black void. Smoke and sound seemed to reverberate from every direction inside the hotel as the soldiers loaded and shot in alternating platoons. Everything was a loud, disorganized mess.[27]

The men from the Michigan battery were incredulous, their eyes fixed downward in a frozen stare. Private Perry Stedman was cradling the head of the nearly unconscious Lieutenant Tyler in his arms. Tyler had been hit in the hands, legs, and chest as he sat outside on the steps. After the first blast, Captain Daly, also wounded, helped Tyler to his feet. As both men turned to enter the doorway, Tyler was struck again under the shoulder blade with a pellet that deeply penetrated his torso. The lieutenant's clothes were saturated, as if he'd been outside in a red rain. After the initial turmoil had subsided, Hale came back to check on his wounded partner. He bent down and asked Perry how Tyler was doing. The nineteen-year-old boy from Lenawee County, Michigan, barely moving in the darkness, whispered into Hale's ear that Lieutenant Tyler was dead. He was the first soldier and only officer in Battery F to be killed in action in the War Between the States.[28]

Quite finished outside, the three snipers left the cemetery and trotted the few deserted city blocks to the woods where they had tied their horses. The men leapt to their mounts and rode off into the night, the sound of random musket fire pouring from the top-floor windows of the Union barracks behind them. The night raiders followed the thin white arc of the moon suspended over the opaque Kentucky landscape all the way to

George Craighead Hatchett's farm just outside Niagara, Kentucky, some ten miles away.

George Hatchett was a fifty-year-old native Virginian and a well-known Southern sympathizer who, with his wife and three children, had made a prosperous farm and family in the bucolic town south of Henderson. Hatchett was "one of Johnson's warmest friends." When the three riders arrived, the owner and his family were away visiting relatives. To compound the temporary confusion, Hatchett's slaves mistook Owen for a Yankee because he was wearing a blue overcoat. A runner was sent to Hatchett with the message that the Federals were after him. Eventually, Hatchett learned the true identity of his visitors and gladly agreed to hide them from the hotbed of Henderson. Johnson, Martin, and Owen were concealed in the nearby woods, so as not to attract attention or indict Hatchett in anything that might later rebound on him or his family. They stayed put for a few days and had their meals brought to them by Hatchett's young son.[29]

CHAPTER 4

Somber Business

At sunrise on June 30, just as the *John T. McCombs* was ready to pull away from Henderson and ply upriver on the New Albany mail run, Captain Ballard got a message that he was to await some government traffic. After hearing hours of musket fire echoing through town the previous evening, Ballard had a queasy suspicion as to why he was being delayed. He idled down the boilers and waited.[30]

When the sun came up on the old cemetery behind the National, the satisfied Union soldiers inspected the grounds and found pools of blood, broken bushes, and flattened grass covering the corner lot. Obviously, the attacking guerrillas had suffered a number of serious casualties. Little did the Federals know at the time, but in their haphazard return fire that night they had actually wounded an old sow that had hauled itself clumsily through the greenlawn before disappearing.[31]

In contrast, it was somber business at the National Hotel. The local undertaker had been commandeered early that morning, and the body of Lieutenant Tyler had been laid in a $70 metal coffin and readied for the trip to Louisville. Accompanying Tyler's body on the *McCombs* were the patched-up wounded from both the Provost Guard and Battery F. Among them from the Provost Guards were Captain Daly, "wounded in the left arm and legs with five buckshot"; his brother Lieutenant Eugene Daly, "slightly wounded in the leg"; Private Charles Webber, "very severely wounded with three shots"; and Corporal Patrick Flood, "severely wounded." From Andrews's Battery were Private Lewis Kiner, "badly wounded"; Edward Barnes, "slightly wounded"; and Private John G. Gould, "flesh wound." Also on board, heavily ironed and under watchful guard by the wounded victims, was prisoner Daniel Griffin, arrested before the barracks attack. To his wounded jailors, "he was a defiant, murderous looking rascal" who would receive due justice in Louisville.[32]

The final casualty count for the previous night's raid was seven wounded and one officer killed. According to the *Henderson Weekly Reporter*, "nearly all received their wounds at the first fire. Besides those wounded there were many others who received shots through their clothes." Johnson's band had fired eleven times. The embarrassing finale had left Union soldiers barricaded inside the National firing blindly at the bushes for more than four hours after the raiders had left the scene.[33]

On Monday afternoon, there was once again a large commotion at the National. Since the beginning of human warfare, enemies have tried to denigrate each other's legitimacy in a war of words that inevitably accompanies the shooting. And so it was after the Sunday attack. As if to punctuate the inherent split in Henderson politics, not one but two fliers went out declaring separate citizens meetings to respond to the attack.[34]

One meeting, to be held at the courthouse building at 2:00 PM, was called by thirty-year-old Henderson Mayor Edwin G. Hall. Ironically, Ed Hall was born in West Point, Kentucky, and came down the Ohio River to Henderson in childhood. After spending time as a young forty-niner looking for gold in California, he came back to Henderson and entered the tobacco business. Hall eventually worked up to the vaunted position of head bookkeeper for Hugh Kerr, Clark & Company before the war. In addition to his tobacco employment, he was a man who had involved himself in community affairs throughout his adult life. In 1859, when the Kentucky State Guard needed a company of soldiers from Henderson, Hall volunteered and was elected first lieutenant. When the company captain resigned in 1860, Ed Hall ascended to the post. He then ran for mayor in the fall of 1860 and unseated "one of the most popular and worthy old men of the city." Hall's ideological loyalties were a mystery to no one; he was a true Southerner who would wind up abandoning office and joining Adam Johnson's recruits within six weeks. When the time came to commence his courthouse meeting that afternoon, he found himself in the uncomfortable position of sitting alone. Not a single person attended his meeting.[35]

The other meeting was called by several prominent city Unionists to take place at the National Hotel at the very time the mayor had set his gathering. At the appointed hour, a large group of Union loyalists symbolically set their footsteps on the stained pavement where the men of the Provost Guard and Andrews's Battery had bled the night before. The ready group voiced Kentucky's fidelity with a strong injection of angry speeches. The assembled men of the city selected a committee of five distinguished representatives to draft a resolution enunciating the sense of the Henderson citizenry. The published text of the resolution was unequivocal. It condemned the attack, labeled the perpetrators "enemies of the human race," and expressed sympathy for the loss of Lieutenant Tyler.[36]

> *Whereas*, We are in the midst of a civil and predatory war, and theft, robbery and murder are being perpetrated in our very midst by bands, styling themselves Southern Rights men; and whereas these thieves, robbers and murderers have been countenanced and harbored by citizens claiming to be sympathizers; and whereas there is no security for the lives or property of loyal citizens while the state of things is permitted to exist,
>
> *Therefore Resolved*, That it is the duty of every loyal citizen to unite in crushing this monster, and restoring community to its original state of peace and order.
>
> *Resolved*, That we will resist, and that it is the duty of the loyal citizens throughout the County to arm themselves and assist the Federal forces in capturing, killing if necessary, and driving from the County every one who has been engaged or may engage in perpetrating these outrages, or who may aid and abet, or harbor these outlaws, and enemies of the human race.
>
> *Resolved*, That we offer our sympathy and condolence to the family and friends of Lieut. Tyler, who was murdered in our city last night by a band of these fiends, and that we deeply sympathize with the wounded officers and soldiers. On motion, the Henderson "Weekly Mail" and all other loyal papers of the Northwest are requested to copy.

J. Lambert, Pres't.
Peter Semonin and Jas. H. Holloway, Secretaries
Col. C. W. Hutchen
John G. Holloway
Jas. B. Lyne
Col. Jas. M. Shackelford[37]
Hon. Archie Dixon[38]

Despite the strong tone of the resolution, even this was not achieved without the perfunctory Henderson debate. The repeated use of the word "loyal" had generated a vocal disagreement among the committee members. The Honorable Archibald Dixon, a sixty-year-old, snowy-haired, lifelong Whig Party politician commonly known as "Governor" (notwithstanding the fact that his highest elected state office was lieutenant governor), wanted the word removed so as not to offend any element in town. The Holloways and Colonel Shackelford emphatically opposed the motion to remove "loyal" from the draft and successfully appealed to the crowd. The Union men of Henderson, after some slight but symbolic disagreement, had officially retaliated with the only thing left them—their anger.[39]

In addition, the *Henderson Weekly Reporter* presented a disquieting rumor. "It has been asserted, we understand, that some of our citizens were engaged or implicated in some way with the fight on Sunday night. This we can not believe." In time, they would.

Back at the Hatchett farm, the three men who brought the true nature of the Civil War directly to the doorstep of formerly sedate Henderson, Kentucky, awoke to relive the experience Monday morning over breakfast. Safely on the far outskirts of town, the men could only guess how the eleven trigger pulls of the previous night had impacted their enemy and the environment of the town.[40]

CHAPTER 5

"Whenever I find you, I'll hang you."

When the *Daily Evansville Journal* of July 1 reached the increasingly busy troop at the Hatchett farm, they became ecstatic. The estimate of the size of the attacking force had far exceeded even their optimistic hopes; it was placed at 150 men. The Louisville newspapers later elevated the number to 500 attackers. These baseless exaggerations did as much to help Johnson's cause as the attack itself. Johnson's men now had the aura of legitimacy needed to recruit a real regiment. For the next few days, there would be a steady stream of convinced recruits putting themselves at Johnson's disposal.[41]

News of the Henderson attack traveled fast in several directions. General Boyle was telegraphed in Louisville the morning after the attack and, after digesting the casualty count and the inflated size of the attacking force, wasted no time sending a message of renewed resolve. Human loss is the grim currency that sustains the black commerce of war, and, for the third time in a week, Boyle sent Union troops to troubled Henderson. He reached for men who were both nearby and tailored for the job, ordering Captain Ben Nicklin and two hundred well-equipped soldiers of the 13th Indiana Light Artillery Battery to board steamers for Henderson. Nicklin, a Pennsylvania-born Abolitionist, was a tough cookie with a simple, focused philosophy regarding the enemy—"Whenever I find you, I'll hang you." His orders were equally simple—"make a final settlement with those who choose to make war on Union troops, whether citizens of Henderson or marauders from the country."[42]

The 13th Indiana Battery was a rare combination of artillery and cavalry, power and speed, suited for and experienced in chasing down guerrillas and projecting an imposing presence. The horse artillery battery had just come off a successful operation against enemy irregulars at the town of Monterey, Kentucky, on June 11. They were now urged to apply their muscle on bushwhackers inhabiting northwest Kentucky.[43]

Within thirty-six hours of receiving his orders, Nicklin and his teamsters were disgorged at their destination. They came off the boat with guns blazing. Nicklin arrived in Henderson after sunset on July 1, just as some Provost Guard pickets had been driven back into town by a group of bandits. After setting up a skirmish line and safely offloading his cannons, the good captain quickly positioned his guns and began bombarding a suspicious-looking nearby woods. In the face of the midnight blackness, he continued to shell the area for more than five hours, leveling everything in sight and sending the town into a worried frenzy. By the time Nicklin signaled all clear, the sky was beginning to lighten with the daybreak of July 2. Thirty-one-year-old Captain Benjamin Strother Nicklin and the 13th Indiana Battery had arrived. Including the small emergency contingent of convalescent soldiers sent from Evansville, the Louisville Provost Guard company, and the Andrews Battery remnants, there were now nearly four hundred active-duty Union soldiers in Henderson.[44]

An update of the ambush on the Henderson National also made its way to Indianapolis. Brigadier General James E. Blythe, a prominent Evansville citizen, politician, and 1st Brigade commander of Indiana Legion (Home Guard) regiments in southwestern Indiana, sent a telegram to his superior, Major General John Love, at the state capital on July 1:

> "There was a fight at Henderson night before last; reinforcements went down last night [from Evansville] partly from convalescents in hospitals. Three or four hundred mounted marauders said to be in Henderson County, further troubles apprehended tomorrow. Our citizens are doing nothing towards defense."[45]

Indiana Governor Oliver Morton learned of the Henderson attack on July 1 while overnighting at his alma mater in Oxford, Ohio. Uncharacteristically, he took no immediate action.

As if to underscore Morton's uneasiness, an ominous message was forwarded to him from Indianapolis on July 2:

> "General Boyle has information that some of the Rebels who were engaged in the affair at Henderson crossed over into our state [Indiana] and thinks they may belong to Indiana. He wants the Legion to route them. He wants Love to go down, but [Love] thinks it unnecessary."[46]

Blythe, in Evansville, later dispelled any Indiana connection to the Henderson attack, but Morton's pensive stance differed from Love's. Morton wanted his Indiana State Legion commander to check the condition of home defenses on Indiana's southern border just in case guerrilla activities escalated further. Though it had been a false alarm this time, Morton had treated the possibility seriously and wanted to be prepared.

CHAPTER 6

Independence Day

Ju23 uly 4 dawned over Evansville, Indiana, much like any other summer
workday; the smokestacks blew black clouds over the city, and the
traffic on the dirt banks of the river bustled as usual. After an early-
morning artillery salute by the Union Battery near the Ohio River shoreline, things seemed commonly normal on road, river, and rail—normal
except for a roaring party-boat celebration that was about to kick off on the
mail packet *Courier*.[47]

Henry Turner Dexter
Reprinted from *Evansville and Its Men of Mark*

Commercial steamship captain
Henry Turner Dexter—a forty-
four-year-old local dockside gad-
about, a native New Yorker, and
part owner of the 258-ton
steamship *Courier*—took the half-
chewed cigar from his mouth,
looked at the party preparations
from the deck of his steamer, and
smiled. There were platefuls of
food, plenty of friends and business associates to partake, and
more than enough appropriated
alcoholic contraband to catalyze a
good time. It was no surprise to
anyone that "those who imbibed
the most seemed to become the
most patriotic." Dexter himself

never touched the stuff, but he understood certain realities and was willing to overlook the behavior of others on Independence Day. Henry Dexter was a staunch Unionist affectionately known as the "gruff, fearless, outspoken, but lovable and bewhiskered speed-demon of the Ohio." He was the type of man who loved life, "forgave his enemies, but not until after they had been hanged…and was a fearless champion of the flag." He was "cool and courageous and seemed to wear a charmed life in the midst of the dangers and casualties through which he passed." There was "no hazard from which he shrank; no toil which he could not endure." He supplemented his king-sized inner passion with a heavy dose of boisterous talk, a little poker, and the occasional bet on the horses.[48]

As the day unfolded, Dexter's dockside Xanadu steamed ahead in the hot sun like the stern-wheelers he cherished as his business. Drinks and dinner were followed by patriotic speeches; speeches were followed by ribald stories; stories were followed by ball games; and ball games were followed by fireworks, ice cream, and (finally) welcome sleep. Even though the typical commerce of southern Indiana seemed to bubble serenely under the vestments of Independence Day, there was a good time to be had by those who knew the right folks.[49]

Some thirty-five miles due south in Slaughtersville, Kentucky, the gears inside the head of Adam Johnson were turning unabated by Independence Day. If anything, the Fourth of July held in his mind the stakes as they were. The struggle for a new day and a new independence was the centerpiece of his life now, and there was little rest and no relaxation for him and his mission. He was still hopeful about the recruiting possibilities, and his band had grown to about ten members. Those who joined told Johnson of like-minded men in their own hometowns, and thus half of his newfound recruits were sent to enlist friends in surrounding counties. The attack on the Henderson barracks also provided Johnson with a second chance to make a first impression. Some who tramped into Johnson's camp had met him earlier in the summer, prior to any of his recent exploits. At that time they had refused to join someone young and untested, but by now Johnson had proven himself worthy of their sacrifice. They came to him ready to put their fate in his hands. Five recruits were with Johnson in Slaughtersville when he received news of Union cavalry stationed in Madisonville, several miles straight south of his early-evening campfire. Tomorrow, his makeshift band would be on the move again.[50]

Independence Day in Henderson signaled the beginning of a slow deterioration in Union military discipline. It was true that the arrival of Nicklin's men had improved appearances, but the Provost Guard had lost its command structure when Captain Daly and his brother were both wounded in the attack on the barracks. Although Lieutenant Hale was still in command of the Michigan soldiers, he leaned almost entirely on Tyler to run the battery. On July 4, James Holloway from Henderson visited General Blythe in Evansville and reported, "Things [in Henderson] are in a very bad condition with soldiers drunk and insubordinate, insulting its citizens without distinction. An officer of sense and nerve is wanted…a suitable commander is of prime importance." Blythe forwarded the report to General Love in Indianapolis with one further bit of intelligence received from a small Indiana river town to the east. "It is reported that guerrillas have established friendly communications with Newburg."[51]

Meanwhile, General Boyle in Louisville still wasn't satisfied with the quantity of troops he was able to assemble in Henderson. On July 4, Boyle asked Indianapolis for more support; "one or two companies" for a short time would suffice. Love transmitted the request to General Blythe in Evansville and was shocked by the reply. Blythe answered, "We have not one organized company here—a meeting last night resulted in nothing, besides, we are threatened here and which men will take arms can be used." General Love, now in receipt of several disturbing communications from Blythe on the same day, saw the wisdom of Morton's orders for him to review matters personally on southern Indiana's border. Love accelerated his arrangements and decided to leave Indianapolis on July 7. On July 5, Love fired one last telegram to Blythe. "Try and organize a company of cavalry. You had better go to Mount Vernon [Indiana] and see what can be done there. Communicate with the company at Newburg, keep me advised." Unfortunately, Blythe was unable to inspect Mount Vernon right away; that visit would come on July 9, after Love's arrival in Evansville. Neither man ever got to Newburg.[52]

As an unknown backdrop to Fourth of July activities on both sides of the Ohio River, another young Confederate cavalry officer was about to make his considerable presence known. He was a man who would rearrange all the puzzle pieces in Kentucky in less than one month. On the same day as Dexter's party in Evansville, a rabble of a different kind was about to part from Knoxville, Tennessee. Equipped with new, sawed-off Enfield muskets, new uniforms, and a new mission, nearly nine hundred men and scouts took to their saddles and headed for parts north. The Second Confederate Kentucky Cavalry Brigade was about to set in motion a series of events that would directly influence the struggle in northwestern Kentucky. The Confederate cavalry officer commanding the brigade was John Hunt Morgan.[53]

Acting Brigadier General Morgan's mission was to confuse and destabilize the quiet Federal backwaters of central Kentucky by overpowering thinly garrisoned areas deep behind the front lines of the western war theater. His grand theme was to underline the idea that Kentucky was a reluctant prisoner to Union military occupation. The by-product hoped for in Morgan's dramatic appearances throughout his adopted home state would be Union prisoners and Confederate recruits. These ideals paralleled those held by Adam Johnson's men, and Morgan's July movements through the center of the Kentucky heartland would eventually allow Johnson to enact his future plans.[54]

CHAPTER 7

The Battle of Browning Springs

B efore daybreak on the morning of July 5, Johnson, at the head of his "band of six," saddled up for the ride to Madisonville, Kentucky. After a morning's ride south on the Henderson–Madisonville Road, his casually clothed band arrived just north of the town of some six hundred citizens and proceeded to reconnoiter the area. Johnson was not without good intelligence on the town's layout; Madisonville was the native home of Frank Owen, his earliest recruit and one of the riders in his troop.[55]

The Union detachment had found the best place in town to encamp. Barely one-half mile west of town, just off Main–Cross Street, was a thirty-foot-high knob upon which a barn belonging to the Browning family was located. Three hundred fifty seasoned cavalrymen, an equal number of horses, one hundred fifty mules, twenty-five wagons, and countless dirty white pyramids speckled the western side of town. On the flattened summit near the main encampment was a small family cemetery that fanned out down the slope to a large, sprawling cornfield running back toward Greasy Creek; west of the creek was dense wood.[56]

True to form, Johnson handled the operation like a professional well aware of his circumstances. After sunrise, the town was inundated with mounted bluecoats, effectively prohibiting any ambuscade near the Federal camp in daylight. Instead, Johnson's men selected a position north of town on the road connecting Slaughtersville to Madisonville. His plan was to surprise a Union detachment headed north once it had cleared the bustle of town and was isolated from help. After a few well-placed volleys, Johnson's squadron would quickly escape north on the main road, arriving in the safe harbor of Slaughtersville. If they were chased, his men could always dissolve into the timbered hills and hollows of friendly country.

The newly supplemented Breckinridge Guards began hacking through the uncomfortable midsummer thickets in preparation for a roadside ambush. Dusty, hot, and tired, the men split into two groups covering both sides of a small section of road; Johnson himself would fire the initial shot head-on into the enemy. The soundless bushwhackers, irritated by thorns and numbed by the suffocating heat, sat coiled for their intended prey until sunset, but no Union riders came.[57]

Adam Johnson had taken on the mission to Hopkins County for several serious reasons, none of which he was willing to give up. His intelligence had indicated that the resident Federal cavalry was on a retribution foray and had authorization to burn and plunder all those known to be aiding the enemy—the enemy being Johnson's contacts throughout Hopkins and Webster Counties. In conjunction with this exigency was the desire to keep the recruiting momentum rolling by adding another notorious success to his expanding list of accomplishments. To leave empty-handed was simply antithetical to his conceived obligations. He would not be thwarted.[58]

Deep into the inky blackness of the early morning on July 6, Johnson took his small band to the foot of the knob where the Federals were sleeping. Six formless silhouettes carefully crept uphill, gently pushing aside cornstalks, weaving among the few sandstone grave markers, and then stopping at the worm-style wooden rail fence surrounding the Browning barn. It was a typical, serene cantonment: tents scattered across the hilltop and soldiers gathered around campfires, playing cards and laughing while wrapped in the invisible envelope of security provided by friendship and numbers. Johnson positioned his men at several fence corners surrounding the camp while he walked quietly around the barn where the soldiers were stationed. Johnson calmly drew to within feet of a seated Union sentinel, brought his shotgun up to his shoulder, and pulled the trigger. By the time the sentry slumped over onto the ground, the barn was abuzz as if a hornet's nest had been cut from its harness. Johnson, a shadowy apparition engulfed in a cloud of smoke, turned and fired again at a soldier running away from the barn. Five black figures raced forward in the night void

"Comanche style," shooting into the tents and yelling as they came. The Federals, stunned and confused, returned fire, nearly hitting Johnson with a shot to the head. A brief, wild firefight was underway with men and bullets peeling in every direction. Within minutes, the Federals scattered to the woods, and Johnson's men fled for their horses. The Battle of Browning Springs was over. The half-dressed Union troops hiding behind the trees of the evening forest were the men of the 1st and 2nd Battalions of the 9th Pennsylvania Cavalry.[59]

A soldier of the 9th described it in his diary:

"We were surprised in camp this morning about 2 o'clock AM by a party of Guerrillas. They came up behind the camp and shot down the guard and then fired into the tents. Our tent is riddled with balls. Henry Feindt who was sleeping by my side had a ball to graze the top of his head but not dangerous. The guard had fourteen buckshot in his legs and thigh. The guerrillas then fled into the woods and made their escape."[60]

The 9th Pennsylvania's commander, Colonel Edward C. Williams, was enjoying a quiet evening's rest in town at the Eagle Hotel. When daylight came on the morning of July 6, the Union cavalry assessed the attacking force to be 1,500 strong. Thereafter, Williams took the precaution of having a company of men protect his personal headquarters every night. Other than a single wounded cavalryman, the end result of the alarming episode was to leave Williams's men shooting nervously at the ill-defined hillside tombstones in the summer nights ahead.[61]

CHAPTER 8

A Diplomatic Correspondence

T he next day, in a small river community twelve miles east of Evansville, the thirty-six-year-old captain of the local Indiana Home Guard company put the July 1 issue of the *Daily Evansville Journal* down on the dinner table and looked southwest out the windows of his spacious, riverside home—a home known in Newburg as the "Old Sandstone Mansion." He had carefully reread the troubling news of the vicious guerrilla attack on the Louisville Guardsmen stationed in Henderson. Out there somewhere was a menace. He silently gave thanks to God for the Ohio River. Although a bit closer, the war was still far away, and there was the immediate commotion of business to tend to at his family warehouse on the waterfront. He had deliveries of wheat to load and knew that things down on the wharf would need his supervision.[62]

July 6 was a busy day for Adam Johnson, too. He spent most of the day returning the thirty-five miles to the outskirts of Henderson with Robert Martin and new recruit Bill Hollis in tow. It was a long ride. The hungry trio stationed themselves temporarily at one of Johnson's numerous safe havens, the John Henry Barrett home on the southern outskirts of town. Barrett was Johnson's uncle and former employer. Adam Johnson had a well-developed network of influential friends throughout the county and beyond. Many of his friendly harbors were older men who had known "Ad" as a child. The commonality of these good Samaritans extended beyond simple familiarity with the young Rebel Johnson. These men, as a rule, were all wealthy beneficiaries of the economic system common to Kentucky in the pre-Civil War era. Many of them also had another important, shared root—they were Virginia natives, steeped in the same heritage that took that state to the very center of the Confederate cause. In divided Kentucky, it wasn't difficult for any viewpoint to find sanction somewhere, and Johnson never went without the willing services of a helping hand.[63]

After the tiring ride north and an evening of telling and retelling yesterday's events, Johnson was handed a copy of the July 3 issue of the *Henderson Weekly Reporter*. For the first time, he took in the full breadth of his National Hotel attack in Henderson. Not only did the newspaper report a detailed account of the ambush, but it also reported on the citizens' meeting, speeches, and resolutions that followed. Johnson's mood darkened. He meticulously digested each word with the careful internal critique of an attorney. He and his men were being dangerously mischaracterized. The difference between criminal murder and a military strike was not an academic one. For the former, the penalty was the noose; for the latter, military parole. But this wasn't the core element of his concern. It was imperative that people throughout the Henderson County area understand that they were opposing an active, legitimate Confederate military presence. This concession must be made explicit.[64]

Johnson decided to enter into a kind of diplomatic correspondence with his opposition using the *Henderson Weekly Reporter* as his vehicle. Because he was almost immediately identified as the instigator of the attack, Johnson understood the resolution for what it was—a communication aimed directly at him. In a brainstorm that was becoming increasingly typical, he decided once again to turn the situation to his advantage. He would demand published retractions from each one of the resolution signatories to be printed in the next issue of the *Henderson Weekly Reporter*. If, as he suspected, they complied, he would have his biggest public-relations victory yet. He took pencil in hand:[65]

Headquarters Breckinridge Guards, July 6, 1862

Noticing in one of the Henderson papers a series of resolutions condoling with the Federal troops on their loss in a recent attack made on them, and denouncing the attacking party as thieves, murderers and robbers—and declaring war on those who made that attack—I wish to thoroughly understand the position you occupy. As it was a portion of my command that made that attack and every man engaged being a sworn Confederate soldier, I conclude that your declaration is against my Government. My orders when I was sent to this department were imperative regarding citizens and their property. I was charged not to molest them in any manner unless they were engaged in war upon us. Now, gentlemen, you perceive why I wish to have a definite answer upon this point. If you are fully resolved to war against us, we will necessarily be compelled to fight you. I have repeatedly said to Union men, who are now living in Henderson, that I did not intend to molest any citizen on account of his politics. I have written to the same effect, and I now repeat it; but I contend that each and every one who signed those resolutions have placed themselves without the pale, and I await an answer to this *to show you what it really means to be an enemy to us.* I deprecate civil war, and have used my best endeavors to avoid coming into contact with citizens; and here I reiterate a piece of advice given to Mr. Delano, viz., for citizens to let soldiers fight their own battles. If they do not wish to see and hear the din of war in their midst, let them have their town cleared of *blue coats* and I will guarantee that no one of them will be molested by Confederate soldiers. I want all persons to know that we are at war with the Federal soldiers, and if they will shut themselves up in houses we will sometimes give them a little fight just for recreation.

Attached to this is a list of names signed to those resolutions, all of whom I consider as having declared war against the Confederate States and each name that I do not find appended to an *article denying that to be their intention, I shall hold him as an enemy and his property subject to confiscation.* The said article must be published in the *Reporter* by Thursday, the 17th of July 1862. All those so appearing shall not be in any manner molested by my men. I have sent a copy of the resolution to the army.

A. R. Johnson, C. S. A.[66]

Johnson reflected on his handiwork and was satisfied. Although it appeared like a brazen challenge to spectators on both sides, the outcome was never seriously in doubt. Johnson personally knew the prominent signers of the petition. He was a lifelong friend of the Holloways and even kept written correspondence with them during his time in Texas. He had also been a friend of Archy Dixon's for years. He knew his audience like his own family, and, as a keen observer of human nature, he knew that a stone-cold threat signed in his own name would command reconsideration. He did not have to establish his credibility with those who read his rejoinder. Johnson's saber rattling rapidly secured the attention of his intended audience. In the sober space of time, the retractions came.[67]

Sixty-one-year-old C. W. Hutchen stated, "No man of common sense could or would construe the action of the citizens' meeting in question as a declaration of war against the so-called Confederate States."

Lambert and Semonin, in a sort of backhanded concession, jointly published a reply. "We did not intend to make war upon the forces of the Confederate Government, nor can we understand how any man of ordinary intellect could so construe [our comments]."

As a political professional, Archibald Dixon's long-winded response declared that the citizens' petition was to "assist in putting down a band of lawless men who…were unauthorized by either the Federal Government or the Southern Confederacy, and who are engaged in robbing and plundering the honest citizens of Henderson County."[68]

Of course, whether Johnson's troop was a "band styling themselves as Southern Rights men" or dutifully enlisted Confederate soldiers was strictly a matter of semantics at the time; the results were the same. By the time the citizens' committee met, they had a heavy suspicion that Adam Johnson was responsible for the attack; they knew he was no rogue outlaw or robber. The committee's fulmination was an emotional response to the idea that the war had arrived on their doorstep, and it was a specific call to join with Union forces to cleanse the county of the intrusion. Johnson's intimidating counter signaled a new reality in Henderson—the new reality being the Civil War in all its true horror.

CHAPTER 9

Nicklin's Dangerous Bunch

By Tuesday, July 8, Union forces had succeeded in making things thoroughly uncomfortable for nearly everyone in the Henderson County area. Nicklin's men had certainly projected a tough stance since their arrival, and anyone in the way could be worse off for the affair. One of Nicklin's hardscrabble lieutenants had been out leading a mounted patrol with seven others just outside of town when a suspicious figure was sighted in the distance and told to halt. Instead, he took off. Without further inquiry, the patrolmen lit out after the presumed guerrilla, unloading their pistols toward the rider as they slowly closed the gap. Finally, a carbine bullet to the head dropped the suspect, and the riderless horse galloped off. Believing themselves to be engaged with the enemy, Nicklin's men carefully cantered up to the lifeless, blood-covered body. They were momentarily frozen by what they found. They had killed a frightened, innocent slave. Although chalked up as another in a string of cruel, embarrassing military mishaps in the area, it did nothing to dampen the perception in Henderson that Nicklin's soldiers were a dangerous bunch.[69]

Nicklin's two artillery sections further intensified the threatening environment by making a flurry of quick but high-profile appearances in the surrounding areas. The Provost Guard chipped in by starting a fairly regular prisoner ferry service between Henderson and Louisville. Whether the situation was met with agreement from the locals or not, Henderson was now an occupied city. Citizens were finding out that even full cooperation with the Federals didn't guarantee security. Anyone in accidental proximity could be subject to the random whims of soldiers on either side seeking food, horses, or fence lumber for an evening fire.[70]

When Republican Governor Oliver Morton was canvassing for a commander of all Indiana Home Guard efforts, he shrewdly selected a Democrat in order to encourage bipartisan support for home defense. The man he chose was John Love. John Love was widely known in Indiana as a man of military substance. He became a West Point cadet in 1837 and graduated near the top of the class of 1841. After a year in cavalry school, he was posted to various frontier forts in western Indian Territory until the mid-1840s. Love served with gallantry as an artillery lieutenant in the Mexican War and was promoted to captain for meritorious service. After a few years as a military instructor and recruiter in the early 1850s, he had spent most of the last decade as a successful businessman.[71]

Following Governor Morton's orders, General Love arrived in Evansville on the evening of July 7 and started out the next day on a series of inspection tours of the assorted Evansville Guard units. Despite the sincere paucity of weapons and trained instructors, Evansville had reported nine active Home Guard companies by October 1861. Love quickly discovered that a quiet spring had reduced them to a paper existence. In response, Love stayed in southern Indiana for almost a week after his July 7 arrival. He prepared a plan for the significant realignment of Evansville's Guard units, calling in the arms of some and redistributing them to others. Love then initiated a series of recruitment and morale-building speeches throughout meeting locations in Evansville. Love and Blythe embarked on an inspection tour of other towns on the border, visiting Mount Vernon on July 9 and planning to visit Newburg in Warrick County later that week. The latter visit would never happen. On July 11, Morton ordered Love to drop everything and proceed immediately to Louisville to confer with General Boyle on Kentucky's new problem: Morgan's Raiders.[72]

CHAPTER 10

The Magnetic Pull of John Hunt Morgan

On July 9, General Jeremiah Boyle, commander of Union forces in Kentucky, received a dispatch from the hamlet of Tompkinsville, Kentucky, that sent a cold shiver from the backs of his heels up to the graying hairs on his neck. That morning after reveille, about 230 men of the 3rd Battalion, 9th Pennsylvania Cavalry, coughed and struggled to their feet as the sun peeked up from the eastern horizon. Soon coffee was brewing, and the men began their daily chores, watering the horses and preparing breakfast. They had been in the general area for more than a month, and this day seemed like so many others. Just last evening, the bulk of the 3rd Battalion, Major Jordan commanding, had returned from an abortive raid on Celina, Tennessee, where they tried to snuff out Confederate Brigadier Morgan and his men. With everyone safely back in camp, the morning calm was rudely interrupted when Jordan spied his pickets rushing in with news that they were about to receive

General Jeremiah Tilford Boyle
Reprinted from
Biographical Encyclopaedia of Kentucky

a visit from their intended quarry, Morgan's Raiders. After a brief but spirited skirmish in which Morgan's "Bull Pups" lobbed a few shells in the major's direction, Jordan found himself cut off from his men and surrounded.

Major Thomas Jefferson Jordan, 9th Pennsylvania Cavalry—along with a good number of others—surrendered into Morgan's hands. The fractured pieces of the 3rd Battalion, 9th Pennsylvania fled, some east to Burkesville, some west to Glasgow.[73]

Boyle knew his situation better than anyone. Kentucky was not a combat zone, and his command consisted of small units scattered across the state. After Morgan pressed on and captured Glasgow on July 10, Boyle sent dispatches to everyone he could think of. By now, Morgan's general intentions were clear, but his strength was not. Boyle assumed the worst—a large force of up to three thousand men collecting recruits like a snowball headed downhill straight for Louisville. He sent dispatches to Major General Don Carlos Buell in Huntsville, Alabama; Union Military Governor Andrew Johnson in Tennessee; Governor Morton in Indianapolis; U.S. Secretary of War Edwin Stanton in Washington, D.C.; Major General Henry Halleck at Corinth, Mississippi; Mayor George Hatch of Cincinnati; Governor David Tod of Ohio; and, finally, President Lincoln himself. His request from everyone was the same: "Send help."[74]

Brigadier General Green Clay Smith had scarcely arrived as the new post commander in Henderson when, on July 11, he received Boyle's frantic message ordering the 13th Indiana Light Artillery and the remainder of Andrews's Battery to Louisville. Just before receiving Boyle's message, Smith had promised Lieutenant Hale that at long last he would have two cannons in town for the Michigan artillerymen within ten days. Hale was ambivalent about the news—he would at last have a proper battery, but it was still ten long days in the future. Now, it was all just another in a series of unfulfilled promises; he was ordered to prepare to board steamers for Louisville. Given all that had happened, Lieutenant Hale wasn't disappointed to be leaving Henderson.[75]

The tragic disaster of Lieutenant Tyler's death had severed a vital link between Hale and his men. Hale had depended upon Tyler for everything; Tyler was industrious, had a good rapport with the men, and was totally loyal to his mentor. With Tyler's demise, Hale had essentially lost control of Battery F. His first misstep was to appoint Lieutenant William H. Brown to be his new second. The men bitterly rejected him, which only served to distance Hale further. After the arrival of the energetic Captain Nicklin, it was almost impossible to keep track of the men at all. Nicklin's hectic countryside raids offered excitement and a sense of purpose. Bored and despondent, groups from Battery F would ride along with either the Provost Guard or the 13th Indiana Battery without permission from their commander. Even though Hale's wife, Louisa, had come all the way from Michigan to visit, he hit bottom when two soldiers failed to answer roll call on July 9. The desertions had begun. Hale blamed his unfortunate circumstance on the legitimate beef that an artillery battery without cannons was an untenable position for everyone. In short, the Michigan men had been let down more by their own government than by any other hardship or external factor. Though glad to be leaving, no one would ever forget his time at Henderson.[76]

Captain Nicklin was issued orders on July 11 to return to Louisville as quickly as possible. Unfortunately, the restless captain was not around to receive the orders. Nicklin, unaware of the apparent urgency created by Morgan in southern Kentucky, had taken the opportunity to plan a quick trip to Indianapolis to give the governor a personal report on his successful suppression of the Kentucky countryside. Nicklin left Henderson on July 10, gave a rousing speech, and showed off some captured booty to a collected throng in Evansville that evening. He then left by rail for Indianapolis on July 11, before Boyle's message to withdraw the battery had arrived at Henderson headquarters. On Saturday night, July 12, the 13th Indiana Independent Light Artillery Battery left Henderson on the *Little Grey Eagle*, the same boat it had come in on. They would never return. In less than a week, Nicklin's Hoosier cannons would be chasing Morgan's Raiders near Paris, Kentucky, some forty miles east of the state capital at Frankfort.[77]

After Nicklin's men left Henderson on the July 12, General Smith felt himself exposed. Smith sent a telegram to the Indiana Legion post commander in Evansville, explaining his predicament:

"On account of the raid on Tompkinsville, Ky. nearly all of my troops have been withdrawn from this post and I feel myself in no condition to resist an attack which I am informed by reliable citizens will be made upon us within a day or two. Therefore, I wish you would send down by the first boat, 200 of your Indiana Legion with at least five days rations so that in case it be necessary I can send them into the country prepared for any emergency. If possible, send them by the first boat. I am sir, your obedient servant, Gen. G. Clay Smith. We have no [local] Legion here and I fear the prospect for organizing is not very flattering."[78]

Smith was desperate. Clay Smith knew that the odds were strongly against Indiana Legion troops crossing the state border, even if such men were available. Time, however, was running out on Union control of Henderson, and there was nothing to lose by asking. He understood, along with nearly everyone else in the Henderson area, what the likely outcome of troop withdrawals would be. Holding orders to the contrary and expecting an attack at any moment, Smith held the Provost Guard and Hale's men at Henderson for one more day while the fate of the city hung in the balance, its inhabitants nervously awaiting the upheaval to come.

At about 3:30 PM on July 14—just before General Smith, the Provost Guard, and the men of Battery F were to shove off on the *John T. McCombs* bound for Louisville—a huge, noisy cloud rumbled into Henderson with nearly three hundred exhausted, dust-covered Union cavalry at its head. General Boyle made it clear that only cavalry would be of serious use in tracking down Morgan, and the only men available to him after the Tompkinsville calamity were the 1st and 2nd Battalions of the 9th Pennsylvania Cavalry, recent recipients of a visit from Adam Johnson's men at Madisonville. With Mexican War hero Colonel Edward C. Williams commanding, the cavalry had responded somewhat leisurely by traveling the thirty-five miles from Madisonville to Henderson in two days. The jubilant Henderson townsfolk had assumed that the Pennsylvania horsemen had come to relieve General Smith's soldiers currently loading onto the *McCombs*. The evacuation of Nicklin's and Andrews's Battery was about to leave the town exposed to angry Confederate retribution after two weeks of intense Union-led anti-guerrilla activity. The cavalry was welcomed with open arms as a symbol of continued stability. The following afternoon, however, they too left Henderson for Louisville. Also on board, in addition to the last load of secessionist prisoners from Henderson, was a citizens' delegation prepared to protest the Federal withdrawal directly to General Boyle. Boyle placated them with empty promises. With Morgan's Raiders still advancing northward, the defense of Louisville was the only thing on Boyle's mind. By July 16, Henderson was once again an open city.[79]

There was one man eagerly watching the developments in his hometown of Henderson, and he was once again considering how the game could come his way.

CHAPTER 11

An Open City

After the Battle of Browning Springs, the 9th Pennsylvania Cavalry remained in the Madisonville area until the evening of July 12. That night, two couriers dashed into camp with a message from General Boyle calling his only available cavalry back to Louisville. Within thirty minutes, the camp came alive with the twin rumors that Major Jordan had been taken prisoner and that the regiment was to move out for Henderson at once. Two days later, the 9th Pennsylvania Cavalry would be watching from the Henderson riverfront as General G. Clay Smith and his men left for Louisville.[80]

Meanwhile, Johnson, who was at Slaughtersville receiving recruits, got intelligence reports on Williams's movements and was satisfied that his supporters would be intact through the second week in July. Union expeditions were sent out from Madisonville almost daily, and some arrests were made, but the thunder surrounding the 9th Pennsylvania's arrival never translated into serious problems for Johnson's network after his attack on July 5.

On July 14, Johnson received a report that a group of Union cavalry headed north was passing under his nose at Slaughtersville on the Henderson–Madisonville Road. Without good knowledge of Morgan's success at Tompkinsville, Johnson interpreted that the bluecoats stationed in Madisonville had either given up or been thwarted in their mission. Either way, with recruiting continuing apace, he counted the evacuation as another victory. In reality, this report was of the victims of Johnson's attack in Madisonville nine days earlier. It was the 1st and 2nd Battalions of the 9th Pennsylvania Cavalry trundling through the countryside on their way toward Henderson. Johnson was not aware that the disheveled "Dutch Cavalry" racing northward ahead of its baggage train was just the beginning of a rapid series of historic events.[81]

Johnson's military force had jumped from about ten soldiers on July 5 to approximately thirty within the next week and a half. By the time Johnson received the stunning news that the entire Union army contingent had left Henderson, he had a very real and growing armaments crisis. If he were to properly outfit a fighting force that would stand up to the well-equipped Union troops in the field, he would need more than the generation-old shotguns that his new recruits were typically toting, if they had anything at all. It was a circumstance that would soon meet head-on with opportunity.

Finally, Governor Morton, after sending several hundred Indiana soldiers to aid Boyle's command in Kentucky, sent a dramatic warning to General Blythe in Evansville on July 14. It was a message that indicated an almost prescient analysis: "The people of the border counties must organize for their own defense. I have no troops that I can send for their defense. I consider the whole border in danger from marauding guerrilla parties." These prophetic words would come back to haunt both Generals Blythe and Love in less than a week's time.[82]

CHAPTER 12

King for a Day

B y midday on July 16, events never before witnessed on the docks of
Evansville began to unfold. Boats from Henderson were emptying
the families of Kentucky Union sympathizers onto Indiana soil. The
political situation in Henderson had become too volatile for many after the
whipsaw of the last three weeks. Those who had helped Union efforts in
snuffing out Confederate activists now feared reprisals. The refugees
appeared in Evansville with the news that Henderson was now open to the
wishes of whatever military power might arrive in town. Most who fled had
no doubt who that would be.[83]

Adam Johnson immediately swung into action. That evening, amid the
silver bullwhips cracking the black sky of a summer storm, Johnson once
again rode to the home of his uncle and former employer. John Barrett filled
him in on the confusing activities at Henderson during the last four days
and confirmed that the town was empty of all Union soldiers; even the
mobile wounded in hospitals had been cleared. Johnson also met with
Phillip Matthews, a member of the Henderson city council, and took the
temperature of political events in town. The city's pending transition was
almost palpable. Johnson decided to send Barrett, a forty-four-year-old
wealthy businessman of the highest honor, into Henderson with word that
his waiting band of Confederate regulars would be taking possession of the
town the next morning. While rumors circulated early on the 17th, the
refugee exodus intensified as the Henderson riverfront became jammed
with people fighting for a place on the *Masonic Gem*'s 10:00 AM schedule for
Evansville.[84]

The drama was thick as Johnson and his troop of forty or so mounted men were sighted cantering down Knoblick Road and entering Main Street. For effect, the riders paused at Third and Main while a crowd began to assemble. Some in the crowd were incredulous, some adoring, and some silently disgusted at what this display of showmanship was likely to mean in the days ahead. Johnson's men then proceeded to the Henderson County Courthouse, where they dismounted and ceremoniously planted the Confederate flag at the entrance gate. Thereafter, the crowd moved on foot to First Street, where their leader announced to the collected throng—citizen and soldier alike—that his men were not to commit an insult, much less any other hazard. Yes, Johnson admitted that many in his group were somewhat unsavory characters, but they were now well under his control and committed to conformity. In effect, the people of Henderson had nothing to fear. Almost as if to punctuate the irony of the moment, the unruly fraternity hastily fanned out to the Hancock House, the hospitals, and other likely locations to collect whatever booty they could find. The few immobile Federal soldiers left in town were quickly paroled and relieved of their weapons.[85]

With the streets nearly empty of Union sympathizers, the morning was sweet redemption for the formerly oppressed Southern administration. A delegation of city officers was sent out to meet the new military commandant of Henderson; many of the men in the group would eventually become comrades in arms. Mayor Hall would become captain (later colonel) of Johnson's Confederate 10th Cavalry, Company A. Twenty-five-year-old, one-armed, wisecracking Henderson County Court Judge Luke Trafton (a friend of Johnson's since his teenage years) became regimental assistant quartermaster of the 10th Cavalry. Phil Matthews of the city council and John Barrett, local millionaire, had calmly discussed affairs with Johnson the previous evening. Although in friendly company, Johnson did not show his hand. He asked if he needed more men to take the town and was assured, no doubt with a wink, that there would "be no fight." Adam R. Johnson was king for a day in Henderson, taking visitors and giving orders throughout the afternoon. His men "put their horses up at the livery stable, and going to the Hancock House ordered dinner. This they got and paid for. They also paid for the keeping of their horses and for other meals which they afterwards partook of." To some in Henderson, it was difficult to tell whether the citizens were hosts to local visitors or subjects of Confederate rule.[86]

From his newly attained position of authority, Johnson, always alert to the public-relations possibilities, took the time to issue a recruiting challenge suffused with the language of grandeur and history that was his style.

Citizens of Kentucky:

It has gone forth to the world that you are a subjugated people—that the iron heel of despotism has destroyed all spirit of resistance and crushed out the last spark of patriotism. The idea has gone through the North, and they look upon you with contempt, and send their hirelings to rule over you. It has crossed the Atlantic, and the eyes of all Europe have been looking at the position of Kentucky with wonder and astonishment. Down in the sunny South, amongst those who ought to be your brothers, you have become a bye-word and a scoff. The Kentucky army has turned their anxious eyes to their native State, and at each new outrage would listen for the tocsin of war; but they have listened and hoped against hope until the last ray has expired. The Confederate Cabinet and Congress have looked for some movement indicating a desire for freedom; but they looked in vain and think Kentucky lost.

But there is one man who has never despaired—that man is John C. Breckinridge—the hero, the statesman and the patriot. With the same never-despairing love that a mother bears to her offspring, does he regard Kentucky—with the same anxious care has he watched her. He asked his government and the world to suspend public opinion until his State should have one more opportunity to redeem her character and now, citizens of Kentucky, the opportunity has presented itself, and for the sake of your former fame and glory—for your country—for your liberties, which ought to be dearer to you than life itself—come to the field! Rally to your country's call! Rise in your majesty and might, and drive from your midst the monster of oppression.

Then prepare now to meet the enemy; send the young men to the field; let them retrieve the character of this once proud and noble State. Circulate through the country that the Confederate Government does not war against the citizens of the country. Can you, with the example set by the people of the South, tamely submit? They have, with heroic devotion, applied the torch to their property, and, with unparalleled unanimity, have they battled for their country. Will you not risk as much as they to achieve your freedom and independence?

A. R. Johnson, C. S. A.
Henderson, July 17, 1862.[87]

News of Rebel-held Henderson spread like a windblown whitecap on the Ohio River. Initial reports were typically outrageous. A virtual brigade of some 1,500 Rebels and three pieces of artillery were at Henderson's doorstep, soon revised to a more modest 800. Later in the day, the number was put at 200, and then finally at "about forty guerrillas who seemed to be enjoying themselves very quietly." By the time things came to reality, the news had already taken on a life of its own up and down the river. Steamers *General Anderson* and *John T. McCombs* refused to leave Evansville on their routine schedules downstream, lest freebooters blockade the river at Henderson. The *Commercial* learned of the news while at West Franklin, Indiana, on its route to Evansville and promptly turned tail back to Mount Vernon. Once at Mount Vernon, rumor also convinced the *Lebanon* to take an early berth.[88]

As the day wore on, all was well for Johnson's expedition, except for the increasing belligerence of one Acting Volunteer Lieutenant Commander Charles G. Perkins on the 155-foot U.S. gunboat *Brilliant*. Perkins, an Ohio native and officer in the Western Flotilla operating out of Cairo, made it his business to patrol the Henderson waters and became a welcome friend to the townsfolk. He had garnered a reputation as a man bound to "respect and protect, not to suspect and destroy." The twenty-five-year-old Perkins had witnessed enough of Johnson's theater and delivered an in-person ultimatum—either take the flag down from the courthouse premises or submit the town to a good shelling from the four 12-pounder cannons on the *Brilliant*. In a show of tension-filled stagecraft, Johnson initially played the cold shoulder, but in the end he didn't know Perkins and couldn't predict what he'd do. Had Johnson known that Perkins's sweetheart, Miss Ann Terry, was living in Henderson, he might have been tempted to call Perkins's bluff. Just before sundown, with nervous citizens (including "Governor" Dixon) warning Johnson of Perkins's sincerity, the flag—along with an impressed wagonload of weapons, canteens, medicine, candles, and blankets—rode off toward the William Soaper farm on the eastern outskirts of town. Although Johnson's one-day intrusion on Henderson would become another recruiting trophy, it was soon overshadowed by events that would hatch a few hours hence. The next day would be a day like no other for the Confederate soldiers in Johnson's Breckinridge Guards. It would be a day that would put him and his men in history for more than a century to come.[89]

BOOK II

NEWBURG, INDIANA

CHAPTER 1

A Shiloh Veteran Comes Home

T HIRTY-FOUR-YEAR-OLD John Hathaway Darby, formerly captain of the 25th Indiana Volunteer Infantry Regiment, Company H, was never happier than when he first saw the twenty-foot-high gravel cliff fronting Newburg, Indiana, on a comfortable spring afternoon in 1862. The steamer he was on slid up to the wharf. Despite being one amid thousands who had come up from the Tennessee River after Shiloh, Darby felt like he was the only person in the world. The white houses terraced among the wooded mound of Newburg were the next best things to heaven. He clambered up to Water Street and noted the familiar panorama of the northward notch in the Ohio River upon which the town rested. Darby scanned east and took in an unobstructed view of the swift, coffee-colored waters that extended past Scuffletown Beach, Kentucky, a mile or so upriver. Off to the southwest, only the newly sprouted foliage on the Kentucky side blocked the sharp river bend.[1]

Hugging the Ohio River just twelve miles east of Evansville, Newburg was a Warrick County, Indiana, town of little more than 1,200 souls in 1862. It traced its origins to 1803, which was an early date for western frontier times. The founding date was true, sort of. John Sprinkle, Darby's grandfather, had founded the town of Sprinklesburg—or Mount Prospect as some called it—in 1803. Nearby, Newburg was founded much later in 1829. Both hamlets lived side-by-side for eight years until they were consolidated in 1837 under the Newburg name. Thus was "Newburg" one of the oldest towns on the lower Ohio River by the time the Civil War erupted.[2]

John Darby, like soldiers of war since the beginning of time, had been looking forward to reuniting with his family since the day he had left for St. Louis with the 25th Indiana in August of 1861. As he walked up the slope to Main Street, thoughts filled his head of how things had been in Newburg before the war. He remembered learning his prewar trade as a carpenter and cabinetmaker by building his own house under his father's tutelage in 1855. He couldn't understand how the joy of working on the porticos and pediments with his father could have been experienced on the same Earth as the wordless horror of what he had seen at Fort Donelson and Shiloh.[3]

Newburg moved in rhythm to the song of the steamboat whistle. In the decade before the Civil War, Darby lived in a thriving town of peak economic importance, and the only worry on everyone's mind was the vagaries of commerce. When Darby was a young boy, Newburg was the busiest port on the Ohio River west of Louisville. The wharves at Newburg were forever in the process of cycling goods from Cincinnati and Kentucky on their way to the Indiana interior, while "lumbering oxcarts filled with beeswax, hay, pork, corn, ginseng root, hominy, beans, tobacco, and feathers" from across southern Indiana funneled down for transport to New Orleans. River trade and transport created enormous wealth for a select few and relative prosperity for many others in town. Darby was one of the lucky ones. It was ironic that two generations of business endeavors had given Newburg stronger ties with the South than with the North. Politically, rural southern Indiana, like its Kentucky neighbor to the south, was bedrock Democratic Party territory in the middle decades of the nineteenth century.[4]

While at its peak in the early 1850s, Newburg, a town that had successfully cast its future with the river for half a century, made a fateful decision. In 1843, 1848, and again in 1851, a rail route was proposed to connect Newburg with the new technology that was changing the face of the American economy. For the third time in eight years, Newburg rejected the railroad. When Evansville signed on to the smoke-belching balloon stacks marching westward in 1852, the future of Newburg as an important economic focal point began to fade. Evansville's population exploded during the late 1850s, and by the end of the decade it was a vibrant city of more than twenty thousand people. To those who had the correct regional overview, Newburg was at the beginning of a long, slow decline. Future growth moved with the rails, and Newburg, for its own reasons, chose not to invest the political muscle to get on board.[5]

When war erupted, young men in Newburg were no different from others throughout Indiana; they almost fought each other to join the army during the initial calls in 1861. Many Newburg locals, including Darby, joined the 25th Indiana and served with distinction in the most serious battlefield combat west of the Appalachians. For those men who didn't enlist in time or who had other obligations to attend, a position in the Indiana Legion seemed like a natural service alternative. In Warrick County, seven Home Guard companies were in action by the end of 1861, all under the titular command of Newburg resident Colonel Daniel F. Bates, 3rd Regiment, Indiana Legion. Three Home Guard companies existed in Newburg, two in Boonville, and one each in Yankeetown and Campbell Township. Each company enlisted between seventy-five and one hundred soldiers, who were issued weapons and drilled to one extent or another. At first, the town turned out with pride to see their men parading in drill. By the spring of 1862, however, the enthusiasm and sense of mission felt by Home Guard units throughout Indiana sagged. As the new year opened, it seemed unlikely that any Confederate force would ever threaten Indiana.[6]

Captain Darby had certainly seen his share of the war. In his first month in the field near Georgetown, Missouri, he and many others in his company had fallen seriously ill when their unconditioned stomachs reacted to a dose of impure river water. It was a rude beginning, but nothing compared to what was ahead. There had been two major battles in the West during the opening twelve months of the war, and the 25th Indiana had been in the thick of both—the capture of Fort Donelson in February 1862 and the bloody carnage at Shiloh, Tennessee, in early April. Few in quiet Newburg would understand the delayed terror of the buzz of an enemy musket ball so close that the hair on one's face moved. Even fewer would understand that the most feared sound in war was the cough that signaled fever. It was all too much; he had seen enough.[7]

Even now, almost a month later, he walked the few steps to his home and remembered things he couldn't explain. He remembered that sunny Tennessee afternoon of April 6 near Pittsburg Landing, but he didn't know whether to tell his wife or anyone else what he had seen. It was in his mind's eye. Above the smoky din, a strange regiment of blue-coated Confederates, a few hundred yards in front, had tried to sneak up on them when the unsuspecting Rebels were attacked from behind by their own cause mistaking them for blue Federals. Just as the 25th Indiana was readying to charge the dazed Rebels caught between hither and yon, a hurricane of soldiers burst through the woods; Brigadier General Benjamin Prentiss's beleaguered men from the Hornet's Nest finally gave way, with the Rebel horde firing on their tails. In a moment, the air was alive with balls traveling in a web around the Hoosiers of Company H. Routed Federals "came sweeping by in utter and total confusion—cavalry, ambulances, artillery and thousands of infantry, all in one mass." If Darby's men didn't move, they would either be trampled by their fleeing compatriots or be surrounded by the eager enemy. But move to where? Twenty-three men, many of them his friends, died that day in Darby's regiment. The 25th Indiana took more than one hundred wounded in every way imaginable, and many, after the choking smoke and smell had cleared, could not be found at all. His own Company H second-in-command was mortally wounded in front of Darby's eyes. Best to leave it all in the past, he decided. In three years, the town would be full of men like him, men who would knowingly pass each other on the street, greet, shake hands, and talk. All the while, underneath would be the secret of the severed body part, the blood-covered neighbor, or the dying comrade's last whisper, "Mother." For now, he carried it alone.[8]

Darby, however, had found someone worthy of admiration in the devil's fire—the 25th's major and Darby's direct superior, John Foster from Evansville. A reluctant warrior, John Watson Foster was a quiet but self-assured "political" officer who had been paid off for his Republican Party service in the 1860 election with a commission as major. Nothing prepared Darby for what he saw of Foster at Shiloh.[9]

The 25th's regimental commander, Lieutenant Colonel William H. Morgan, had been wounded in the leg early that April day and taken from the battlefield. The loss left the regiment decapitated, and fear spread like a wave through the men. Combat leadership devolved unceremoniously onto the inexperienced major. Foster stepped forward and personally planted the flag, hailing the regiment to rally around the colors. With the weight of battlefield command suddenly thrust upon him like the stony Earth on the shoulders of Atlas, Foster was transformed out of necessity. He was "active, brave, and energetic, inspiring his men with courage and confidence." Thirsty, exhausted, and nearly beaten by nightfall, Darby felt the major had shown his mettle under the most vivid extremes that life had to offer. Darby would spend his life trying to forget some things about that day, but he would remember Foster.[10]

CHAPTER 2
The Bethells of Newburg

During the early months of 1862, Legion captains slowly came to an uneasy compromise with an unpleasant fact of life: with every presidential call for Federal volunteers, the ranks of the local Home Guard suffered. And so it was that by spring the men available for service in the Indiana Legion had been so thinned by U.S. army recruiting that two Newburg companies, the Grays and the Warrick Rangers, had been disbanded, their arms safely held-in-wait at a Newburg riverside warehouse. Only the Newburg Home Guard, under the command of Captain Union Bethell, maintained enough strength to call itself a company in the immediate Newburg area.[11]

The aptly named Union Bethell was a prominent thirty-six-year-old merchant and Warrick County native who, with his older brother Thomas, traded tobacco, flour, cotton, and other goods on the Ohio as far as Cincinnati to the east and New Orleans to the south. The storied Bethell family traced its origins all the way back to the arrival of James Bethell on the vessel *Safety* at Jamestown, Virginia, in 1635. Since the earliest days of the fledgling nation, each family generation had poured honor and obligation on the next by accepting the risks and rewards of military service as the centerpiece in their lives. In 1753, William Bethell, Union's great-grandfather, became lieutenant of Augusta County, Virginia, Foot Infantry and then, in 1755, a captain in the Virginia State Militia. When William moved to Guilford County, North Carolina, he once again served as captain, this time in the North Carolina State Militia during the Revolutionary War. William's sons, Sampson and John, Union's grandfather and granduncle respectively, also fought for the patriot army in the pivotal battles of Kings Mountain and Cowpens, returning to the plow after independence was secured. The next generation saw Union's father, Cloud Bethell, serve in Larkin Ferrell's Company, 7th Brigade, West Tennessee Militia Infantry in the War of 1812 against Britain.[12]

In Union's own generation, brother Thomas had been appointed colonel in the Indiana State Militia in the early 1840s and received the training that would set the foundation of his imposing military career. When Congress urgently authorized ten new volunteer regiments in February of 1847, Thomas stepped forward as organizer and captain of a company of Warrick County citizen-soldiers to serve in the war against Mexico. Thomas had certainly earned the title "hero" during his time in service.

In March of 1847, Thomas Bethell's Company I, 16th U.S. Infantry Regiment, boarded a steamer in Louisville for basic training in New Orleans. Measles broke out almost immediately. A third of his men perished in the first month. After their four-week basic training was completed, the 16th U.S. boarded ships for General Zachary Taylor's main supply base on Brazos Island at the mouth of the Rio Grande River. Equipped with flintlocks, black powder, bayonets, and the assorted accoutrements of war, Bethell's men were taken up the Rio Grande and then marched overland to the U.S. encampment in central Mexico at Camargo. More than a thousand miles from home and surrounded on all sides by the inscrutable foothills of the Sierra Madre Mountains, the Newburg men moved south from Camargo in the summer of 1847. While trudging across the hot, desolate roads, they were subject to ambush by hostile *rancheros* at any moment. By the time the men finally arrived at Monterrey, most of the fighting in the immediate region had ended. The 16th U.S. Infantry settled into the role of an occupying army in conquered territory. The men quietly served on provost guard duty in and around Monterrey until the war's successful conclusion. Thomas was in Federal service for a total of 382 days during the war and earned thirty cents a day for the trouble.

Thomas Bethell's Home
Photo date unknown
Courtesy Kay Lant

For a second time, Thomas was called into state service and was once more commissioned colonel in the Indiana Militia in 1853. Now in his mid-forties, Thomas again agreed to serve as captain of a Newburg volunteer company headed for war. He was commissioned captain of Company I, 25th Indiana Volunteer Infantry Regiment in the summer of 1861.[13]

After the death of his father, Cloud Bethell, in 1844, pioneer merchant Thomas Floyd Bethell became the family patriarch. He was a man well equipped with the ambition to lead a frontier family to success. Between the years of his military service, Thomas had married twice, built his own home, had five children, founded the successful businesses that would secure the family name, and served as Newburg town trustee. Although a freethinking supporter of women's rights and an Abolitionist, he was elected as a Democrat to the Indiana State House of Representatives for the 1857–1859 sessions. By 1862, Thomas's counsel was sought by businessmen, politicians, and military authorities throughout the state and beyond. He wasn't just the head of the Bethell clan; he was the elder statesman of the entire town.[14]

It was difficult for the younger Union to get started in the long shadow of his older brother, and he still had no firm occupation or direction by the age of twenty-four. It wasn't until Union got married at the relatively late age of twenty-seven that he began to authoritatively take his place in Newburg, getting involved in Thomas's businesses while he was away and joining the new Republican Party. Since then, Union's stature had grown, and he was now a sizeable cog in the Bethell brothers' success.[15]

The Bethells owned a host of businesses and properties that made them the economic and political center of town. They were farm-produce dealers and had a steam-driven flourmill. The brothers owned a general store, a pork house, a tobacco warehouse, a coalmine that serviced the needs of the river steamers, and a cooperage that could produce the one hundred barrels a day needed to package their goods. The small entrepreneurial family hub embedded in the center of the expanding American nation had merchant contracts as far away as New York and Liverpool, England. Their trading businesses alone transacted more than $100,000 annually by the time of the war—an enormous sum for the age.[16]

At home, Union was a dutiful family man with wife Eva, three children, two domestic maids, a male servant, and two clerks under his roof. Union was a gentleman of substantial wealth in 1862, and, as such, he was a man who felt responsible for the well-being of the community that was connected to his good fortune. Within this grand context, Union Bethell, a late-bloomer who had rarely left Warrick County, carefully stepped into service as company captain of the Newburg Home Guards.[17]

By the summer of 1862, Newburg had seen its share of the war. Like everywhere else on the Ohio River, Newburg had received its fair allotment of grisly wounded and stiff dead from the feared hospital boats that arrived after Shiloh. In early June, there were more than three hundred impaired soldiers populating every extra inch in town.[18]

Citizens' committees were established for the care of the wounded, and honor guards were offered for the services of the dead. Newspapers advertised for donations of time, clothing, and food, while local women's groups organized for the purpose of fabricating the never-ending reams of bandages needed to heal the horrible wounds of war. The town dedicated itself to meeting every need of these brave souls (many of whom were Hoosiers) who had given and then lost a measure of themselves to save the treasured nation. In mid-July, there were still approximately eighty-five convalescing sick and walking wounded put up at the two makeshift hospitals in town—the Exchange Hotel and the smaller hospital annex at the home of the Frame family. Union Bethell had not just given himself to the leadership of the Home Guard; he was also the dominant force in these benevolent endeavors as well. If someone wanted to know or do something in Newburg, the Bethell brothers were the men to see.[19]

Union Bethell had kept himself faithfully informed of local events and was certainly aware of the perplexing situation caused by Morgan's Raiders in Kentucky. There was no doubt that roving opportunists had taken advantage of Morgan's handiwork in order to create havoc for their own benefit. But by July 18, it seemed clear that Newburg was not among Morgan's immediate intentions. And as much as things seemed to be falling apart in Kentucky, matters in everyday Indiana seemed quietly and gratefully removed.

CHAPTER 3

Deadly Conspiracy

On April 28, 1795, barely a generation after the founding fathers declared independence, William Soaper was born in Loudon County, Virginia. Young Soaper spent his formative years in Virginia and then moved to Henderson County, Kentucky, at age twenty-five. There, he spent time as a traveling saddler moving through small towns nearby, plying his trade. Soaper hit it big when he got into the tobacco business with Judge Thomas Towles, one of the most influential and trusted men in Henderson. Soon, Soaper's hard work, integrity, and charity made him a community leader and a rich man.[20]

On Thursday night, July 17, 1862, William Soaper (now sixty-seven years old and a wealthy patriarch in a family of eleven) was an unprepared host to nearly thirty ecstatic members of the Confederate Breckinridge Guards. A well-known, well-off conservative Democrat and native Virginian, Soaper was not necessarily a Confederate sympathizer. If anything, his politics were that of a pragmatic businessman. As such, he understood his position in the sudden, uneasy occupation of his farm. Johnson needed someone with enough space and food for a large number of hungry men and horses; whether his hosts were Union or Confederate wasn't an issue while he was in possession of a small company of armed soldiers. Unannounced and unwelcome, they and their mounts were quietly accommodated as best as could be managed. When Johnson sent an offer to pay for the food and supplies used by his men, Soaper wisely declined. Finding little in common with Soaper, Johnson set up his personal headquarters at the farm of Soaper's neighbor, former Deputy Sheriff Elijah Worsham. Meanwhile, the elated Breckinridge Guardsmen built cooking fires, ate, laughed, divvied up the equipment and guns, and told of their adventures in wonderland all evening. They had pulled a literal *coup d'etat* for a day and were now casually enjoying the moment. Their relatively unmolested eight-hour appearance in Henderson had sent Yankee refugees scurrying, had locked up river traffic between Mount Vernon and Newburg, and had sent shock waves through the community.[21]

Later that evening at the Soaper farm, Johnson learned he had three new men in camp who had followed his band during their retreat from Henderson; their names were Elliott and Andrew Mefford, father and son respectively, and "Hamp" Carney. After Johnson himself, they would become the most important figures in the Newburg story. Without them, it is unlikely the raid would ever have happened.[22]

Elliott Mefford was a fifty-five-year-old Kentucky native, a Newburg resident, and a family man who made his livelihood trading locally on both sides of the river; Andrew was Elliott's twenty-year-old son, his eldest. That evening, Elliott Mefford patiently told Johnson about the state of affairs at the unsuspecting Hoosier town. Mefford had been a resident of Warrick County for more than twenty years and knew Newburg well, particularly that the Bethell brothers reigned at the center of the town's power structure. Elliott Mefford had been one of Newburg's Mexican War heroes serving under Captain Thomas Bethell in the late 1840s. Staring at the evening fire and with the smell of wood smoke all around, Mefford related how several hundred weapons from decommissioned Home Guard units were sitting unguarded in a riverside warehouse. He also gave insights into local routines and told of convalescing Union troops in a makeshift hospital at the Exchange Hotel. Henry Hampton Carney II, the twenty-nine-year-old Newburg wharfmaster, told Johnson about riverboat activity and shared that the next afternoon's schedule would be clear at the Newburg dock. The group also discussed the utility of nearby Scuffletown, Kentucky, in a possible plan to raid Newburg and take the weapons. Most importantly, Johnson was given a rundown on the local Home Guard and its inexperienced commander.[23]

Johnson considered their story. The Henderson occupation had furnished enough weapons to outfit his troops, but it wouldn't be long before he'd need more. This would be a risky operation at best, one that would have to be thought through. How and when would he get his men across the river? How would they secure the Union soldiers in the hospital? How would they neutralize the Home Guard? What about telegraph service to Evansville? What was the political disposition of the community townsfolk?

Even with these serious questions, the allure of a successful raid on Indiana soil had at least two strong potential positives for him—the first being the likely recruitment windfall that would follow, and the second being the weapons themselves. Johnson was no stranger to the Indiana shoreline, having traveled across the Ohio often as a child. Maybe it wasn't so far-fetched. Deep into the night, Johnson and the conspirators continued to discuss the issues back and forth. Increasingly, Johnson saw the feasibility of the operation. As long as the treasured element of surprise remained on his side, he felt his chances were good. Johnson understood that he had to act fast. Newspaper reports of his foray into Henderson would be widely distributed by July 19; after that date, Indiana Legion companies would be on alert. Late that evening, he decided to go ahead with the Newburg raid.[24]

CHAPTER 4

Stovepipe Johnson's Confederate Raid on Newburg, Indiana

To the bewilderment of his men, Johnson ordered the Soaper bivouac struck in the pre-dawn hours of July 18. Including the Meffords and Carney in the lead, about thirty mounted men spilled out onto the moonlit landscape and headed east on the Owensboro Road. Within minutes, the men came upon a crossroad and turned north onto an ancient dirt path that led them through various black, swampy twists and tangles to the confluence of the Green River emptying into the Ohio. Upon arriving at the mouth of the Green, the nightriders were welcomed by the summer sun rising behind the local ferryman who carried them across on flatboats. At midmorning, after passing the scattered sycamore, sweetgum, and pecan trees of the "Point," the horses finally stopped, and a dust cloud faded over the tree line on the river bank. They were at the isolated riverside community of Scuffletown, Kentucky, across from Newburg, Indiana.[25]

A hamlet of perhaps one hundred subsistence farmers and fisherman, Scuffletown had richly earned its name as the result of numerous moonshine-fueled backwoods fisticuffs in frontier times. The twelve thousand fertile acres of the peninsula east of the Green River where Scuffletown was located was undeveloped land more like that of the eighteenth century than the 1860s. There were a few scattered churches and a physician or two; even the Henderson staple, tobacco, had barely taken root by the time of the war. With sparse, stilted, ramshackle housing scattered among the small tilled fields, in Scuffletown it was quite strange to see anyone other than a neighbor, much less thirty armed, mounted soldiers. With Mefford and Carney as their local ambassadors, Johnson's Kentucky raiders were welcomed. As they dismounted and collected in groups, rumors were rampant; Johnson still had not detailed the operation.[26]

Carney recommended attacking at noon when the dock would be clear and the townsfolk would be safely in their homes taking lunch. No alarm would be sounded, and there was no danger from the river. Although the Ohio was receiving a welcome bump in the water level from recent storms, it was still pathetically low even for this time of year. With luck, the men could have walked across without getting their chests wet. The telegraph to Evansville was Johnson's primary concern. One short telegram could quickly bring hundreds of men from Evansville to Newburg. Not yet known to Johnson, the telegraph had been knocked out by the same thunderstorms that recently had raised the river, and the source of the problem had yet to be found. Superior intelligence and secret intent were once again on his side; he now added the luck of the stars.[27]

Johnson, Martin, and the conspirators walked back to the Breckinridge Guardsmen milling around behind the tree line next to their horses. It was time for one of Johnson's inspirational calls to duty. He spoke with his usual dramatic sense. "Soldiers, as soon as you reach the other side of the Ohio, you will be standing on a powder magazine, and cowardice would be the match to ignite it. All who are willing and confident take a step to the front." Johnson's compact oratory had the intended effect. With the challenge stated thusly, he left the men with no real choice; they all stepped forward.[28]

The plan was revealed. Johnson, Frank Owen, and Felix Eakin would launch themselves on an innocent-looking skiff and land like simple businessmen in front of the Newburg warehouse. Martin and the others would commandeer the Scuffletown–Cypress Beach ferry, along with any other vessels necessary to transport the mob, and start out for Newburg a few moments before Johnson touched Indiana. The advance party would carry several jugs of flammable liquid. If Martin's squadron faced opposition upon arrival, Johnson would begin to light the town afire by shooting burning materials onto the roof shingles of nearby houses. If the conflict became desperate, Johnson and his men would hastily abscond across the river with whatever guns they could get while setting the

Bethell arsenal ablaze to cover their escape. Before any of this could happen, however, Johnson let the men in on the grand military deception that would cover their activities that day. They were to fabricate two decoy cannons using wagon wheels, a section of stovepipe, and a black charred log. The faux battery would be trundled out to an open spot below the Scuffletown beach just before they left Kentucky soil and would loom over Newburg, freezing any attempt at counterattack during the raid. Johnson was to play his largest gamble yet; the bet was the lives of himself and his men.[29]

By midday, all preparations were in place. Twenty-seven-year-old John Patterson and a close friend, seventeen-year-old Jerome Clarke, had fabricated the sham cannons by rolling a blackened log and an old section of stovepipe each onto a set of wagon wheels. The raiders' horses had been gathered near the cannons in clear view as a show of force to the other side, and Martin was in place with the ferry fleet. Johnson took off for the warehouse, shotguns concealed in the bottom of the boat. In less than fifteen minutes, the three intruders landed at the foot of State Street, scrambled up the steep slope, and ducked inside the open doors of Bethell's two-story brick warehouse. As promised by the conspirators, the idle weapons were in plain sight. The men began to bolt themselves inside. It was quite a haul—approximately "200 muskets, seventy-five sabers, and 130 pistols with holsters, still in their original boxes."[30]

Martin's group took off, and a small flotilla made its way quickly toward Newburg; they were not unnoticed. Standing on the Indiana shoreline and observing the unusually crammed ferry as it made its way downriver was none other than former U.S. Army Captain John Hathaway Darby, now retired from the 25th Indiana. Darby squinted in the gathering midday haze. No doubt about it—it was certainly strange to see that many men packed into a ferry headed hell-bent for Newburg. Something was up. Also with Darby down on the waterfront was U.S. Army Sergeant Henry. Henry concurred, strange indeed. The two of them continued to stare, transfixed, at the oncoming horde.[31]

As if there weren't enough spectators watching the unfolding invasion, Henry and Darby were soon joined at the foot of Sycamore Street by thirty-six-year-old Dr. John R. Tilman, a prominent resident and veteran of the 60th Indiana. Tilman had been assistant surgeon for the 60th, but he had been forced to resign in May of 1862 after only three months' service due to a crippling injury. By July, he was home and once again practicing medicine. Without any other formal command structure, the doctor was nominally in charge of the eighty-five-or-so convalescing soldiers in the two converted hospitals in town. Tilman took one look at the river and had no trouble figuring out what was going on—a band of robbers was about to sack a defenseless Newburg. It was his worst nightmare. Several times during the summer, Tilman and Legion Colonel Bates had discussed arming the soldiers in the event of an emergency, but nothing ever came of it. Now they all would pay.[32]

Tilman, in deference to Darby's former rank, turned and asked him to take command of the soldiers in the hospital; Darby refused. As of April 20, Darby wasn't a soldier of any rank and didn't feel he had the authority or inclination to take command. At Darby's suggestion, the doctor then turned to Sergeant Henry, still a fully attired active member of the U.S. Army, and asked him to take command of the soldiers in town; Henry agreed. Meanwhile, precious minutes passed before the riverside debate was finally settled. By the time Henry agreed to take charge, Martin and his men were about to beach their craft on the sand and gravel-strewn bluffs of Newburg, almost at the feet of the three conversing Indianans.[33]

It was all too late for any defense of Newburg. Johnson's unassuming Confederate triad had no trouble finding the Bethell building—Union Bethell's name was painted in tall white letters on the wall facing the river. The band of three had scrambled up to the structure unnoticed by anyone. Johnson already had barricaded the doors of the warehouse and was on his way to the Exchange Hotel just a few dozen yards uphill at the southwest corner of State and Jennings. Darby, Henry, and Tilman fanned out to begin warning the town. With two dozen of Martin's plainly dressed rank-and-file making their way rapidly up the bluff to the east end of town and with Johnson striding toward the sandstone-and-brick hotel that contained the bulk of the recovering soldiers, the Newburg contingent would arrive just moments late at every turn.[34]

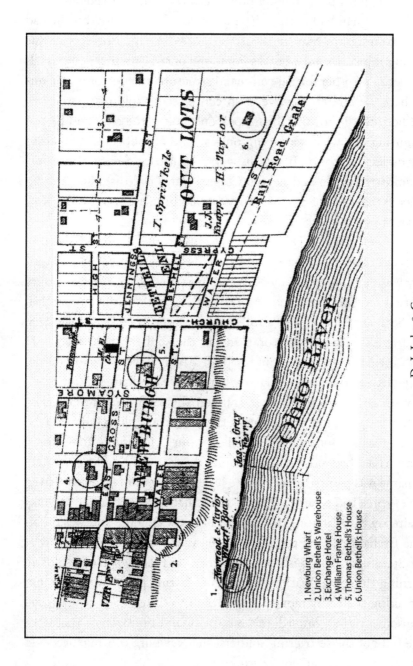

D. J. Lake & Co.
Map of Newburg, Indiana, 1880
Edited

1. Newburg Wharf
2. Union Bethell's Warehouse
3. Exchange Hotel
4. William Frame House
5. Thomas Bethell's House
6. Union Bethell's House

Johnson, alerted by suspicious foot traffic at the Exchange Hotel hospital and not knowing exactly what he would discover, burst into the hotel to find a mass of soldiers on the ground floor, fifteen with muskets in hand. He didn't know the muskets were as yet unloaded. Tilman had entered the hotel only seconds before, and the soldiers were just in the process of breaking out their gear. Everyone in unison now stared in disbelief as Johnson entered with shotgun in hand. No one doubted that his gun was loaded. Johnson authoritatively strutted toward the muzzles pointed at his chest inside the Exchange, pushed the gun barrels aside, and announced that the town was occupied and resistance was useless; anyone who should surrender would not be harmed. In the event a little vinegar was needed to tame his audience, Johnson then added that "if a single cap was fired, the last man to whom he was addressing himself would be massacred." In the flicker of hesitation that hung between the opponents, a miracle happened. On Tilman's orders, the soldiers began stacking their arms. To the almost audible beat of Johnson's pounding heart, the men disarmed and put themselves at his disposal as prisoners. He herded them upstairs into a large dining room and told them to keep quiet.[35]

The Exchange Hotel Hospital at Newburg, Indiana
Photo date unknown
Courtesy Kay Lant

No sooner had this episode subsided than another crisis came from nowhere—the burly Sergeant Henry bounding up to the second floor by way of a noisy wood staircase on the exterior of the building. The Orderly Sergeant swung the door onto an almost unbelievable scene—there inside the dining room stood every last one of the hospitalized soldiers, dejected and forlorn, and a single Rebel held an old double-barreled shotgun in his direction.

Reflexively, Henry shouted, "What are you doing? Where in the hell are our guns!"

Johnson answered indirectly. "Move another step, and I will riddle you with bullets."

A seemingly endless pause ensued as Henry and Johnson stared into each other's eyes.

A voice rang out. "They've got all the streets guarded, and are coming this way."

Like vapor leaving a balloon, Henry exhaled and surrendered. Johnson, now in charge of Union troops at Newburg, gave his prisoners a choice to come with him as captives or to get the muster rolls and prepare to accept Confederate parole. They all chose parole.[36]

After surrendering the men at the Exchange, Tilman slipped away in the confusion and took off for the Frame House to warn the thirty-or-so soldiers there. Though it was only a one-minute walk, he never made it to his destination; a Confederate picket was posted just ahead of him on Jennings Street. The unarmed soldiers at the Frame place were already in Rebel custody. Tilman made an immediate left-hand turn up State Street, running north toward Boonville to get help and warning houses in the country along the way. He returned to Newburg at the head of three hundred armed men by sunset. To his astonishment, he would soon be arrested for his part in the raid.[37]

Martin arrived just after the climactic showdown at the Exchange, his men now picketing the neighborhood. Despite the initial threat of a loud, pistol-waving Harriet Knouse—Pennsylvania wife of Union Corporal Henry Knouse, who was still in the field with Darby's former company—in less than twenty minutes, it was over. Or was it? Johnson had possession of the weapons, the soldiers would soon be paroled, armed pickets had secured the area, and a wagon team would shortly be hauling the booty down to the waiting river craft. With the confused citizenry milling about, some in the streets, some glued to their windows, yet another tentacle had come out to threaten the raid. Johnson was informed that Captain Union Bethell was down on Water Street talking intently to several men who were quickly trying to fill him in on events. An Indiana Home Guard company was about to be called out to perform its intended service for the first time since the start of the war.[38]

The "Frame House"—known now as the "Rutledge House"
The hospital annex on the day of the Confederate raid
Photo date unknown
Courtesy Kay Lant

Bethell sent out a runner to call the troops into town. Johnson, on hearing news of Bethell's arrival, left the remainder of the parolees in the hands of Martin and Patterson and hustled down to the river. By the time Johnson walked up to Union Bethell, the Hoosier captain was being held at gunpoint by a couple of the raiders, but he was still talking to several citizens gathered around him. Johnson, now sweating in the midday heat, pushed his way straight to Bethell and spoke without introduction. "Gentlemen, I hear that there is a Home Guard near town that is about to attack me, and I must say that I came here to get these guns, I have them, and I propose to keep them; I want nothing more and do not intend to disturb any of the citizens or any of their property, but if I am hindered or fired on, I'll shell this town to the ground." All those within earshot, Bethell included, reeled in disbelief. With Johnson's audience rapt, the final card was played. "I see, sir, that you have a field glass and by looking across the river you can see that I am prepared to carry out my threat." Every head in the riverside gaggle turned at once to view what appeared to be a menacing artillery battery upriver on the far side. Bethell had been outdrawn. Under the circumstances, there was little that could be done. If all Johnson wanted was the guns, they could always be recovered or replaced. To call Johnson's bluff wasn't worth the possibility of cannon balls cutting the women and children of Newburg to pieces. From where Bethell stood, the cannons seemed as close to his home as they were to anything else of importance. Union Bethell, suddenly pale and trembling, glanced eastward in the direction of his home where his wife and children were huddled and then reluctantly sent out a countermanding order for the Guard to stay outside town—at least for the time being.[39]

In full agonizing view of Union Bethell and the collected citizenry of Newburg, the raiders began loading up their booty. To Bethell's resigned disgust, several Newburg villagers came down and gave willing aid, while others began to converse merrily with the enemy. Water and whiskey were served to the thirsty Rebels amid the background noise of wagons loaded with military hardware rattling through the streets. In his heart, Bethell knew the possibilities. In the last twelve months, the demographics of Newburg had changed dramatically; it was now a town of women, children, and older men. Most young male Union sympathizers were off serving in the army, leaving Bethell with the raw kindling ready to be lit afire.[40]

For the second time in twenty-four hours, Adam Johnson's promise to harm neither person nor property turned out to be half true. Once feral instincts had been unleashed, they could not now be contained. With things firmly under control, Johnson's men began looting the town. Johnson, a civilian adventurer with no formal military background, was a loose, convivial commander. He held an empathetic ear to the habits of his gritty Kentucky quiltwork of ruffians and independent thinkers. He was no disciplinarian. Therefore, when his men began to plunder the townsfolk of Newburg against his wishes, he simply busied himself with the military object at hand, neither sanctioning nor stopping the roving opportunism of his men.

Again with the help of several Newburg citizens, the Rebels rustled some horses and were guided to houses containing foodstuffs, blankets, clothing, and other valuables that could be carried away. Once rumor got around that the Rebels were looting, the Slaughter family, in a scene repeated throughout the ages, collected up the family silverware, took it to the woods behind their house, and buried it. Not knowing how long the Confederate occupation was going to last, some families packed their belongings that afternoon and left town like refugees. Other families fled eastward and piled into the Old Sandstone Mansion and locked themselves in. One woman, who hadn't yet heard the news of the Confederate takeover, stepped out onto the road toward the grocery store and was stunned to see a young, armed picket stationed at the stone wall bounding the street corner. "When the man turned his head, the woman recognized him from visits across the river. 'What are you doing here, Phil Hicks?' she said. 'Nothing except guarding your town,' he responded, and then with Kentucky gallantry, he added, 'We didn't come here to molest the ladies. Pass on!'"[41]

Sardonic wit, the humanly mundane, and the sudden shock of war swirled together during the oppressively hot, sticky afternoon. In a moment of ironic humor, a raider stole $50 from a citizen, to which the citizen notified the raider that it was not customary to steal money during a military operation. The raider replied that he would leave some newly acquired Confederate property—medicine, clothing, and furniture—in the Exchange hospital for the citizen and that he was welcome to help himself to it in payment once the Rebels left. At one point, the horse of Jesse Fuller from Boonville was about to be taken when a Southern accent said, "Jesse's all right." As quick as that, Jesse was spared. More than spared, Jesse collected some stolen coffee for himself. Before it was over, one lucky raider increased his accounts by nabbing $100 in U.S. greenbacks from the hospital. But by far the most common picture was of terrified women and children glued to slightly parted curtains throughout town as the armed, unkempt strangers walked up and down the steep dirt streets of Newburg, sizing up the possibilities in each house as they went.[42]

The final symbolic act was the ransacking of the Home Guard captain's house. Union Bethell's home was broken into, and anything of value that could be carried was taken out. Even Bethell's favorite mount, "Old John," was confiscated. Among the men who pillaged his home was a raider named John Patterson.[43]

The "Old Sandstone Mansion"—known now as the "Old Stone House"
Union Bethell's home on the day of the Confederate raid
Photo date unknown
Courtesy Kay Lant

CHAPTER 5
The Bird Has Flown

B y early afternoon, word was getting around that something extraordinary was on display. Folks from Scuffletown, charitably holding the raiders' horses, were spectating the event. But news was also headed west. With the telegraph out, there was only one way to communicate the urgent need for help to those who could give it. Union Bethell's brother-in-law, fifty-one-year-old Dr. Eli Lewis, grabbed his horse soon after the attack began and headed out onto Newburg Road streaking for Evansville. By 3:00 PM, he was at the Evansville Courthouse at Third and Main, where he tied his horse before scaling the steps. The horse collapsed dead. Undaunted, Lewis went up and started frenetically explaining the shocking events to anyone and everyone who would listen.[44]

Lieutenant Colonel John Watson Foster, veteran of Fort Donelson and hero at Shiloh, on leave in Evansville from the 25th Indiana, was summoned as the most prominent local citizen and senior Union army officer in town. Though quite young, Foster was a well-known and highly respected man in Evansville. A Pike County native, Indiana University class valedictorian at the age of nineteen, Harvard Law School alumnus, and Abolitionist Republican go-getter for Lincoln in 1860, the twenty-six-year-old was the type of man who could wield authority given almost any situation. He happened to be present strictly as a result of the unfortunate circumstances of war. His brother-in-law, eighteen-year-old Second Lieutenant Alexander McFerson, acting commissary of the 25th Indiana and a soldier for barely two months, had died in LaGrange, Tennessee, of typhoid fever on June 27. Foster had just finished the heartrending business of escorting the body home to his wife's family for burial. Colonel Foster, now standing in full uniform on the same courthouse steps upon which he had nominated the Lincoln–Hamlin ticket to the citizenry of Evansville in 1860, immediately sent runners out to the U.S. Marine Hospital on Ohio Street and to the newly opened Military Hospital. All able-bodied men, including all available Home Guardsmen, were to come prepared to respond to the emergency. The local artillery defense batteries were also summoned and rattled their way down to the river. Within an hour, a disorganized mob of a thousand men and three field artillery pieces were assembled on the sloped dirt bank of the Evansville riverfront. Women, children, and assorted spectators were stretched across every crowded inch between Sycamore and Locust streets; it looked like all of Evansville had turned out for a parade.[45]

The Evansville, Indiana, courthouse
Late Nineteenth Century
Courtesy of the Special Collections, Willard Library

Three steamboats had put in at Evansville that afternoon, staging themselves for their regular packet run either to or from Cairo, Illinois. Little did they know that their names were about to enter history. Among the first to be contacted about the dire condition upstream was none other than Union patriot Henry T. Dexter on the stern-wheeled *Courier*. Dexter could barely believe his luck; he had been waiting for the opportunity to feed some shot to the Rebels ever since his close call at Paducah with a "super-heated rabble" who took objection to him flying the Stars and Stripes through western Kentucky. Dexter had taken the precaution of arming his steamers with a single 6-pounder cannon on a forecastle swivel. It probably saved his life at the Paducah wharf. The chance to use it in the name of country was now at hand. With the fresh success of the Mississippi Ram Fleet in mind, Dexter declared that if he needed to use the *Courier* as a ram, he would. A little before 5:00 PM, the *Courier*, toting a squadron of infantry and an armed crew and accompanied by the side-wheeler *Commercial*, was bound for Green River "flying light and running for glory." The strategy was to cut off the escape route of the Rebels by closing off the Green River crossings, thus sealing the enemy on the peninsula created by the Green and Ohio rivers. It was a good plan.[46]

Back at Newburg, Martin's improvised ferry fleet was now nearly filled to the gunnels with muskets, ammunition, swords, pistols, sugar, coffee, blankets, candles, horses, hospital supplies, various and sundry small items, and even a pair of ice skates. Perhaps the strangest item loaded aboard that afternoon was an old milk cow. While at the riverfront, Martin had appropriated two additional flats that had been tied up to the wharfboat on their arrival. There were now a fair number of craft ready to take off for Kentucky, including one carrying the wagons that would be used as getaway vehicles on the other side. Any weapons that could not be carried off in good order would be rendered useless by either breaking them up or dumping them in the river. As 5:00 PM approached, the increasingly nervous Rebels were wrapping things up when the bugle call to assemble the scattered pickets was sounded. With Martin just pushing off on the last loaded boat, Johnson and his two shipmates, Owen and Eakin, got into their craft and started for Kentucky. They wasted no time making their escape; they "made the water foam" on their way across. By the time Johnson was halfway over, the Home Guard was swarming the Newburg hillside.[47]

It was slightly past 5:00 PM when Adam Johnson, standing on the soil of the Kentucky bottomlands opposing Newburg, detected the black issue of steam stacks coming up from Evansville. It wasn't hard to guess where the steamers were headed. The group split up. Martin, his loaded wagons, and the bulk of the raiders took off for a private ferry upriver on the Green. Unable to reach the ferry at the mouth of the Green before the steamers, Martin's men would now need precious time to get away clean toward Slaughtersville. Johnson took Jack Thompson, "Tennessee" Julius George, and John Patterson, and the men rode as fast as they could for the mouth of the Green River. Johnson had one more card to play in his gambler's hand.[48]

At the last possible moment, Johnson arrived and sent Patterson on the ferry across to the point on the western side of the mouth; George and Thompson would take cover in a hastily erected "Indian thicket" on the east point. Once again, Johnson's superior familiarity with the terrain came to his rescue. The channel at the mouth of the Green River ran tight on the east point, a fact that Johnson was about to exploit. He instructed his men to wait for the rapidly oncoming steamers until they followed the channel in to a position near shore where the men were hidden. Once in range, the raiders were to jump out of the bushes and fire at the overcrowded deck of soldiers on board, in hopes that the steamers would turn back out onto the Ohio, creating confusion and chewing up time needed for Martin's escape.[49]

Captain Samuel Archer piloted the *Commercial* in on cue, swinging close to the eastern point covered in thick brushwood. Just as the boat came past McAllister's Landing, inside of fifty yards from the bank, shotgun blasts rang out from the bushes. One ball hit a passenger, and another passed through the gangway. Johnson's gambit churned to perfection as the *Commercial* turned back onto the Ohio, covering its retreat with small arms while allowing the *Courier* with its swivel gun to come forward and level fire at the point. The Rebel escape party at the mouth of the Green skulked off in the underbrush.

By 6:00 PM the 183-foot, side-wheeler *Eugene*—which carried two companies of convalescent soldiers, a section of the Union Battery, and Colonel Foster—came onto the scene and sighted both preceding vessels "laying to" with the *Courier* spitting fire into the bushes. Covered by the *Courier*, Captain Tom Dusouchet, known in Evansville as the "Ancient Mariner," slowly eased the *Eugene* into the Green River. Laboring under the misconception that the attack at the mouth of the Green signaled the presence of the entire Rebel force, the *Eugene* carefully swept its way past the point and traveled about a mile upriver, where it disgorged a company of soldiers onto the eastern shoreline. The troops strung themselves in a line across the peninsula to head off the escaping raiders, but "the bird had flown." Martin, with more than an hour head start, had taken a more direct route to points upriver on the Green and was already behind the line. He safely led his rickety amphibious cavalcade back to the Slaughtersville environs. For them, the raid was over.[50]

CHAPTER 6

The Ugly Face of an Angry Mob

W hile the *Courier* was expending the last of its ammunition on the foliage at the mouth of the Green River, things were taking a sinister turn at Newburg. The townsmen who had sided with the raiders that afternoon were now staring into the ugly face of an angry mob. Before Johnson and his self-styled commandos had touched back onto Kentucky soil, Newburg was filled with earnest-looking legionnaires bent on retribution. Victims of sin would now have their way. Hamp Carney, the Newburg wharfmaster who knew the dock would be clear during the afternoon hours, was readying to take to the water when, for the first time all day, a blast sounded, and a billow of white smoke marked the spot. Carney was shot dead in the street. He was left in the exact spot where he had fallen, pooled in his own blood, for several hours before being thrown into a wagon. His lifeless body was displayed on Jennings Street into the evening hours.[51]

Elliott Mefford, perhaps the most instrumental figure in the entire raid save Johnson himself, was also shot, but apparently this alone was not enough. After accepting a slug, he was rushed with a bayonet, and Mefford's twisting body bent the metal spike while inside of him. Miraculously, he remained alive and was taken for care.[52]

Arriving too late to do much good at the mouth of the Green, the Union men of Evansville were in no mood for reconciliation. An armed landing party from the steamers stepped ashore and questioned the ferryman who had shuttled Johnson's band toward the east earlier that morning and taken John Patterson back before the arrival of the Evansville steamers. The ferryman's own wife identified him to be a Southern sympathizer. That information was more than enough for Henry Dexter to claim his prize. The ferryman was arrested and taken back to Evansville aboard the *Courier* with his confiscated flats in tow. The time was 8:30 PM.[53]

With the *Courier* and *Commercial* now headed back to Evansville, the *Eugene*, still with more than a hundred soldiers and a cannon battery on board, emerged from the Green River and made its way toward Newburg. When the *Eugene* arrived as the mid-summer sun was going down, the town had swelled to one and one-half times its everyday size. Between six hundred and seven hundred men had poured in from the Warrick County countryside, lugging every manner of weapon known at the time. All those who lifted their hands to help the Rebels were rounded up. Several wayward citizens including local sawmill owner James Myrick, Augustus Huff, and Democratic newspaperman John Frary escaped Newburg that night, never to return.[54]

Lieutenant Colonel Foster arrived on the scene and was mobbed by a kinetic populace all aflutter to give their version of events. To begin with, Foster was pointed in the direction of the beached fleet used by Johnson's crew in their getaway just across the river. The *Eugene* passed over and rounded up the boats, towing some back to Newburg and scuttling others. Once back on shore, Foster began interviewing Newburg residents about the day's events. John Foster knew Newburg well—many members of his regiment came from the town, and some were even in the hospital during the showdown that afternoon. It wasn't difficult for the army colonel to find people he could trust to give him the straight story.

It was shocking; he could barely believe the truth of it. Indiana had been invaded with nary a shot fired in defense. It was true that one man was dead and another seriously wounded, but both were traitorous Newburg residents who had been shot by a local Home Guardsman. Compounding the enormity of the event was the evidence that at least some Newburg residents appeared to have participated willingly in the looting. This was the most difficult part for Foster, and those responsible would pay. He began boarding the alleged traitors; George W. Ayres was loaded up along with fifty-year-old farmer John Hurst and thirty-two-year-old farmer William Lee. Also in detention was hard-line Georgia Democrat and Newburg grocer Solomon Coker, who bitterly denied all traitorous claims. Boonville lawyer Jesse Fuller was no longer "all right"; he was arrested too. Andrew Huston, the forty-four-year-old Kentucky native and longtime Newburg inhabitant who had eagerly helped load muskets onto the Confederate flats, was arrested and escorted aboard. General Blythe in Evansville, while looking for coverage in the confusion and accusations that flew thick that night, had poor Dr. Tilman, U.S. Army veteran and chairman of the first meeting to organize Newburg's Home Guard company, arrested and assigned responsibility for the hospitalized soldiers' surrender. As midnight passed, the *Eugene*, with the glow of lit coal ash flying up from her boiler stacks, pushed off the wharf at Newburg and drifted downstream to Evansville like a dim torch floating on the black liquid of the Ohio. July 18, 1862, was now history.[55]

On the morning of July 19, Elliott Mefford, shot and stabbed, was brought out on an iron hospital lounge in front of the Exchange Hotel. The intention of the angry citizenry was to assert immediate justice on their hometown traitor by means of an impromptu trial. It never got that far. Before proceedings could begin, twenty-five-year-old Ira Duncan, Warrick County veteran of the 14th Indiana Infantry, took his household squirrel gun in hand, walked up to Mefford, and shot him point blank in the head in front of the collected crowd. With the gruesome, bloody punctuation of near decapitation from a short-range rifle ball, immediate affairs in Newburg resulting from the raid were over. Duncan was arrested for murder.[56]

On the same day as Mefford's execution in front of the gathered Newburg public, the *Indianapolis Daily Journal*, short on facts but long on caustic, gave voice to the passions of the overheated political element in the state capital:

> "We are at length brought to realize the shameful fact that our own soil is not safe from bands of rebel robbers. They are this morning plundering our farms and murdering our citizens. For the first time during the war a free State has been polluted by the foot of the enemy. Indianans, how long shall this disgrace be borne? These robbers are in our power. They can be taken and

killed to the last man. None should ever bear to the Southern bank of the Ohio the disgraceful news of their audacity. Arouse and arm! Let us teach these thieves and murderers a lesson that will keep them away forever. No party strife can separate us on this subject. We are all Hoosiers proud of our State, proud of the honor she has won, and rightfully proud. Shall we suffer the shame of invasion, and not write our vengeance in the blood of the invaders? Fill up the ranks. Pour out the regiments, and we will repay this insult a thousand fold, and no squeamish sense of former ties shall spare the wretches who have perpetrated it. Revenge is dear to all. In this cause it is holy. It is our duty to revenge the insult and exact a bloody reparation. For every drop of Hoosier blood spilled in this invasion, let us have a rebel life. For every dollar plundered, let us lay waste to a rebel farm. Make the war terrible to those who have invoked it. It is time. Let us act bravely, promptly, and effectively."[57]

BOOK III

EVANSVILLE, INDIANA

CHAPTER 1

Governor Morton Takes Charge

O N AUGUST 4, 1823, OLIVER HAZARD Perry Throck Morton was born into the small, rural settlement of Salisbury in the rugged eastern county of Wayne, Indiana—it was a town that had already seen its best days. The isolated, declining, ten-family community delivered the first Indiana governor born on Hoosier-state soil; in a few years, Salisbury would be gone forever.[1]

Indiana Governor Oliver Perry Morton
Reprinted from *Soldier of Indiana*

Before Oliver Morton turned three years old, his mother died, and the young child was shuttled to Ohio where he was raised to his early teens by two doting, widowed aunts. "Perry" developed into a "quiet and undemonstrative" boy whose large frame drew him to athletics. Steeped in Biblical studies, the most notable characteristic attached to the awkward youth in his Ohio years was his affinity for books and reading.[2]

The Wayne County Seminary opened in 1837, and Oliver was returned to Indiana to take up formal study. "Ol," as his classmates called him, stayed on for one year and distinguished himself as a "good-natured, big-souled boy" and a favored debater. Like Adam Johnson, Morton found employment as an apothecary's assistant after completing his elementary education. The trade was unattractive to him, and he soon quit. After an equally unhappy interim as an apprentice hatter, Morton collected what money he had inherited from his grandfather's estate and enrolled himself in Miami University at Oxford, Ohio.[3]

"In 1844, on the day of the Presidential election, a young man of large frame, with high forehead, dark eyes, and straight hair, rather overgrown in appearance and with clothes that fitted him none too well, rode into Centreville [Indiana] upon a gray horse bespattered with mud." After two years of college in Ohio, Morton triumphantly returned to the county of his birth, launched a career as a lawyer, and entered politics as a steadfast Democrat. Morton worked hard on behalf of Indiana's Democrats until he dramatically broke with the party over the subject of slavery in the mid-1850s. While casting around for a new political affiliation, Morton was chosen to be a delegate to the preliminary convention of the new Republican Party—he had found himself a home.[4]

In 1856, the unlikely Morton was selected to be the Republican Party candidate for governor of Indiana. In the campaign that followed, Morton introduced his slow, forceful, unadorned style of oratory to the voters of Indiana. He was a man who declaimed in blunt tones, paring away all metaphor and humor. The bare, convincing manner became his lifelong trademark. His basic campaign premise was to isolate slavery where it had taken hold while prohibiting its extension to the expanding American territories. Morton lost the gubernatorial election of 1856, but he left behind an investment that would pay dividends in the future. He had organized a new, credible political infrastructure in the state of Indiana.[5]

Morton again found himself on the Republican ticket in 1860, this time as candidate for lieutenant governor under party leader and Mexican War veteran Colonel Henry Smith Lane. When the Indiana Republican Party swept to a surprising, landslide victory in both the Indiana State General Assembly and in the governor's race, a previously conceived political bargain was set in motion. Because state legislators picked their prospective U.S. senators under the rules of the national constitution at that time, Henry Lane resigned his office as governor and instead was chosen United States senator by the new Republican Indiana State Assembly. It was by this quirk that Oliver Morton ascended to Lane's vacancy in the governor's chair. Much like the election of a one-term Illinois congressman to the presidency in the most troubled time since the American Revolution, somehow fate had found O. P. Morton at the moment he was needed most.[6]

Governor Morton first learned of the Newburg raid when a telegram arrived in Indianapolis from Legion General James Blythe in Evansville. Dexter's steamer fleet was still chasing the Rebel escape when Blythe sent off the first few words to the governor: "Newburg taken by guerrillas— Evansville threatened." From that moment on, Morton took control of the military response to the raid. Once Adam Johnson got the attention of Governor Morton, he now had an opponent with the will and resources to destroy him.[7]

Despite the initial sketchy reports, the thirty-eight-year-old, balding, heavy-set Indiana governor began dictating orders. On the evening of the raid, Morton and Blythe exchanged a steady stream of telegrams discussing updates on the ground and Blythe's requirements to repel the attack. Blythe needed men, weapons, and a gunboat. Morton took the kind of aggressive action that launched Newburg events into a new phase. The Hoosiers would now have their turn.[8]

Within minutes, Morton had formulated a plan. His most urgent business was to put the largest Union force he could find into Henderson; this in turn would improve the security of southern Indiana. It wouldn't be easy. Not only had recruiting efforts been underway for two weeks in response to President Lincoln's call for 300,000 three-year volunteers, but also Morton recently had sent more than 400 fresh Indiana troopers to Kentucky to help General Boyle. Despite all Morton had done for Boyle and the U.S. Army, the governor once again found himself drawing on the patriotism of Indiana volunteers. Searching for Union recruits, he sent telegrams to his trusted contacts throughout the state.[9]

After hastily updating Secretary of War Stanton in Washington, D.C., Morton's second and somewhat ironic communication was to General Boyle hinting for Kentucky soldiers and gunboats. Boyle, now enjoying the benefit of hundreds of Indiana soldiers in repelling Morgan's Raiders, craftily forwarded the plea to Brigadier General William K. Strong, com-

mander at Cairo, Illinois. Morton followed up later that evening by sending his own telegram to Cairo requesting a gunboat from Ohio River Fleet
Captain Alexander Pennock.[10]

General Strong, back on duty after a lengthy recovery from a life-threat-
ening accident, rapidly assembled 150 soldiers from the 63rd Illinois
Infantry. Strong then took the initiative to poll Brigadier General Quinby
in Columbus, Kentucky, for any help he could offer. Quinby collected a
grab bag patchwork composed by every man he could get his hands on:
"Company A, 20th Battalion, 16th U.S. Regulars, sixty men; Company H,
13th Wisconsin, forty-eight men; and Stenbeck's Battery, 2nd Illinois
Artillery, twenty-five men." The 63rd Illinois would await transport from
Cairo on Pennock's boats as soon as the fleet captain could be contacted.
Quinby's men would make their way to Evansville on the steamer *Rob Roy*
from Columbus.[11]

Fleet Captain Pennock, ill and asleep at Mound City, Illinois, could not
be reached on July 18 because the telegraph operators had turned in for the
night. Left with a clear emergency on his hands, spunky Cairo U.S. Army
Quartermaster George D. Wise convened his own late-night four-man
impromptu war council consisting of the limited hodgepodge still awake—
a naval gunner, one of Wise's own clerks, and Captain Getty. Possessing no
available gunboat, the makeshift command decided unanimously to rig up
the newly captured 268-foot transport supply steamer *Clara Dolson* with
four 12-pounder rifled howitzers and to send the armed tug *Restless*. While
the steamers were coaled and stocked, the last of Cairo's provisional military
command turned in for the night.[12]

Early on the morning of July 19, the newly appointed General-in-Chief
of the Union army, Major General Henry Halleck, arrived at Cairo by
steamer from points below. Immediately, an artillery salute was ordered in
his honor. Amid the wild rumors and preparations of the previous night,
the sudden pre-dawn cannonading sent local townsmen to battle stations
as citizens were rousted from bed assuming the city to be under Rebel
attack. Captain Pennock, still at Mound City but hearing the thunder of
guns from Cairo, nearly burned two steamers at the Mound City dock to
keep them from falling into the enemy's hands. In time, the confusion sub-

sided. Quartermaster Wise's improvised fleet orders were ratified by Pennock, who hustled to the Cairo wharfboat to command the assemblage. The two-boat fleet, stocked with Strong's men, left Cairo on the evening of July 19 and arrived in Evansville by 6:00 AM Monday, July 21. For Morton, it was a start.[13]

As far as the gunboat was concerned, the resourcefulness of Evansville post Assistant Quartermaster Lieutenant Francis H. Ehrman came in handy. By coincidence, one of the strangest U.S. warships to come up the Ohio River eased onto the landing at Evansville the night of the raid on its way to New Albany, Indiana. The name of the vessel, oddly protected with stacked bales of cotton and straw, was *T. D. Horner* under the command of First Master Robert Dalzell. It was part of the now-famous Mississippi Ram Fleet. The fleet was designed to be thrown at the opposing navy. It was a concept as old as Caesar.[14]

The Ram Fleet was the brainchild of Charles Ellet, Jr., one of the top engineers in the United States for decades prior to the war. Ellet had gotten the ear of Secretary of War Edwin Stanton and persuaded him to fund the purchase and refitting of a fleet of ships under the personal command of Ellet, who would report only to Stanton. The highest rank Stanton could grant without Senate approval was colonel. Thus was an army colonel set upon the western river waters in charge of a naval fleet. Because the rams were outside any normal command structure, both army and navy shunned them until they proved themselves by bringing victory in the naval Battle of Memphis on June 6, 1862. Since then, their reputation was of ships that were willing to plunge headlong into places where few others dared. Even though the *Horner* was only a supply ship for the main ram vessels, it was well outfitted and had a heroic cachet by association. It drew a crowd at the Evansville wharf.[15]

Of course, all this was unknown to Lieutenant Ehrman—all he knew was that General Blythe wanted to get his hands on a warship to help with activities in the Henderson–Evansville area. If Fleet Captain Pennock couldn't send a gunboat to Evansville, the *Horner* would have to fit the bill. In the names of General Blythe and Governor Morton, Ehrman directed the ship to remain at Evansville and await orders.[16]

CHAPTER 2

Anxious for a Fight

Governor Morton's office became the nerve center for the Newburg response team, busily exchanging dozens of telegrams between far-flung communities throughout the state. Among these was a telegram from General Blythe in Evansville notifying the governor that Colonel Foster had returned from Newburg with prisoners. With news still evolving in the state capital, Morton naturally would have assumed the captives were Rebel raiders had Blythe not supplied the unusual clarification that they were "citizens of the town." By this time, Morton was already aware that a Newburg doctor had been arrested for "order[ing] them [the convalescent Union soldiers] to lay down their arms," but he had not yet learned the complete extent of the traitorous behavior demonstrated by some wayward citizens in Newburg. Eager to participate in the interrogation, Morton initially ordered the prisoners to Indianapolis, but he changed his mind and had them held in Evansville when he decided to make an on-the-scene visit himself.[17]

Throughout the Friday evening of July 18, news of the fall of Newburg radiated from Indianapolis "on the wings of lightning." On July 19, Governor Morton issued a call for thirty-day volunteers to any community that was able to respond. The reaction was characteristic of Hoosier men. Two men from the town of Greensburg—Colonel James Gavin, home on leave from the 7th Indiana, along with the enlisted help of Colonel John T. Wilder of the 17th Indiana—informed the governor that same day that five hundred men from Decatur County had volunteered within four hours. It was a heroic effort considering the enlistment drive already underway. Morton, mentally juggling his forces, instructed Gavin to send his men to

92

Indianapolis, where they would be assigned to guard Confederate prisoners at Camp Morton while he reallocated his U.S. Army guards currently in town to Kentucky. Gavin replied that his men would "rather go to Kentucky and make prisoners of the rebels." Gavin's men were conveyed to Indianapolis, where they were hastily outfitted and then treated to an unanticipated breather at the State House grove for a Sunday afternoon of insightful political speeches. Thereafter, the volunteers were bundled aboard the rails for Evansville, where they arrived before daylight on Monday morning, July 21.[18]

Another surprising telegram landed on the governor's desk early on July 19, this one from Captain Melville D. Topping in Terre Haute. Topping volunteered his eighty-man company to Morton for immediate action; it was another in a series of small miracles. Morton knew Topping was the commander of the Union Rifles of Terre Haute. The Union Rifles was an independent company, meaning its men had spent their own money on equipment and had trained on their own rigorous schedule. Topping wanted the Kentucky mission and even offered his help in raising an additional company of soldiers from Terre Haute. Despite violent thunderstorms that saw "a column of livid fire rise out of the far southwest to span the whole heavens in one broad lurid glare," Captain Topping's command "arrived in this city [Evansville] Saturday evening and elicited much admiration and praise for their fine soldierly appearance and their admirable drill. Of their subsequent movements it would not be proper at present to speak. They are anxious for a fight, and it would afford them ineffable pleasure to meet Adam Johnson and his band of rebels." Indeed.[19]

Topping's supplemental help came in the form of the Terre Haute Rifles, a company made of stout German folk and convalescent soldiers. They were noted as being "a robust, athletic sort of men, and include Justices of the Peace, hotel-keepers, provisioners, thrifty mechanics, etc. They are all fighting men and are rapidly perfecting themselves in drill." There was no time to send the new Terre Haute soldiers to Indianapolis for outfitting. Instead, Morton would send a stock of uniforms and guns directly to Evansville, and units needing supplies could outfit there. The

German company left Terre Haute on Saturday morning and outfitted themselves in Evansville that same evening.[20]

Later on July 19, Morton began receiving telegrams from General Love, now on the scene in Evansville. Things were moving quickly, and Love arrived to a confusing prospect. Soon, hundreds of Indiana soldiers would be invading Henderson County, and important administrative matters had yet to be settled. Were these men members of the Indiana Legion, or were they U.S. Army soldiers? If they were army regulars, who would lead them? Certainly, Love had no authority to send Indiana Home Guard troops into Kentucky, but he also did not have the authority to command U.S. troops in his role as Legion commander. Morton conferred with General Boyle, and the two of them came to a gentlemen's agreement. In the wake of the emergency, the suddenly tough-minded Boyle allowed Indiana soldiers to operate freely in Kentucky with one condition: the Rebels were to "be shot—nothing else will do; I do not want such prisoners."[21]

After the Union Rifles had taken dinner at the Evansville Courthouse on the evening of July 19, they were given orders to report to the riverfront and board the armored, stern-wheeled ram *Horner*. In an hour's time, the swift steamer arrived at Newburg to the sight of dozens of armed, ominous men lining the shore at the ready. Newburg was taking no chances. The *Horner* was carrying a cargo of guns, caps, and ammunition to reinforce the greatly expanded Newburg defense corps. Waiting on the dock to receive the weapons was Home Guard regimental commander Colonel Bates. The *Horner* remained overnight at the Newburg wharf with the Union Rifles spread everywhere on deck under the stars.[22]

At 3:00 AM on July 20, all on board were called to arms as the fire in *Horner*'s boiler furnaces was brought up, and the steamer drifted away from the Newburg dock and headed for Green River. Pulling up the Green, *Horner*'s noisy paddles pushed the steamer past the first lock on Green River toward the bluff where the town of Spottsville was located. At Spottsville, the Union Rifles formed up and went ashore to interrogate the locals concerning Johnson's troops. Citizens confirmed that Martin's Newburg wagon train had crossed the Green five miles below Spottsville on the evening of July 18, but nothing had been heard from them since.

After breakfast on board, the Union Rifles slowly drifted back downstream on the *Horner* until they saw two men skulking in the brush. Once again, the Union Rifles went ashore, swarming the banks with blue, and they caught up with the two men in a deep-woods cabin. They were not a part of Johnson's gang. After returning to Newburg for a quick stop, the *Horner* steamed safely to Evansville. At the very least, the word was out; the Federals were on the scene in force.[23]

CHAPTER 3

Rumors of Rebels

As the curtain rose on the third full week in July, news of the Confederate raid on Newburg shook the entire Ohio River valley. For the next several weeks, southern Indiana fought the twin phantoms of fear and imagination. The illusory cocoon of safety provided by the Ohio River had been easily punctured, and now the enemy seemed to be everywhere. Word came that the guerrillas were in force south of Mount Vernon, ready to rush across the Ohio and take the town. General Blythe sent runners west from Evansville only to find everything at peace in the sleepy riverside village. It was alleged there were three hundred Confederate insurgents at French's Island staged to cross the river; Rockport, Indiana, was reported occupied; and a harrowing transmission that Boonville had been taken and burnt to the ground flashed across Daviess County. In Kentucky, a large group of Rebels was spotted in the Green River bottoms, a formation was gathering at Morganfield, and the first lock on Green River was destroyed, trapping steamers *Mattie Cook* and *Lue Eaves* above. A strong Confederate force was sighted across from Mound City, Illinois, where several Federal gunboats were under construction. Although these rumors were all false, the dangers had proven all too real at Newburg, and no one was underestimating anymore.[24]

In a more sober reaction, the Cannelton, Indiana, Home Guard inspected its idle armory and found itself with thirty or forty extra Springfields, which were moved into the hands of new volunteers. Princeton, Indiana, overnight, raised a new Legion company even though they were thirty miles north of the action.[25]

Typically, Hoosiers are slow to anger; however, the raid had triggered a deep and widespread indignation. "The people of the state were aroused, and abandoning their plows, and their threshing machines, they demanded guns." President Abraham Lincoln had called for three hundred thousand volunteers just two weeks before the raid, and the ranks of the regiment designated to satisfy the local commitment were slowly expanding. The Newburg raid significantly boosted recruitment and the 65th Indiana, forming at Camp Gibson, Princeton, went from two hundred men before the raid to a full complement of one thousand by the second week in August. When recruits continued to pour in, the governor decided that he would not turn them away as he had in the past. Newburg had upped the ante.[26]

Johnson's raid had made the premise real; the War Between the States was now a matter that had become personal to homes on Indiana soil. The raid did more to boost recruitment than all the Indiana politicians and generals combined. Although Morton didn't take any satisfaction from the Newburg events, he wasn't going to discourage the loyal Hoosier reaction.

CHAPTER 4

A Union in Kentucky

◆◆◆

Morton's hastily convened expeditionary force assembled in Evansville during the daylight hours of July 21. The formerly quiet, industrious city of peace and commerce was abuzz with the dramatic new influx of soldiers and sailors. This Monday morning was like none other. The *Daily Evansville Journal* reported: "Our city is full of distinguished military gentlemen and the gleaming of bayonets and the glinting of gold lace gives the place quite a military appearance." Besides generals Love and Blythe, there were four U.S. Army colonels, State Attorney General John F. Kibbey, and three Western Flotilla navy captains in town. Lesser officers were "as thick as quails in August." Evansville's response to Johnson's raid would be the only major combat operation hosted by the city during the war.[27]

Governor Morton also came to Evansville and became thoroughly absorbed in overseeing the gathering military activities. The governor, with generals Love and Blythe in tow, then turned his attention to reassuring the local population by delivering a "soul-stirring speech on the steps of the Washington Hotel, depicting in glowing colors the duty of citizens on the border in this great national emergency." Perhaps it was coincidence, but while General Love was in town his previously recommended reorganization of the Evansville Home Guard, neglected to this point, now saw great activity. The Vanderburgh Grays and the City Guards held recruiting meetings, and drill was back on regular schedule.[28]

The rapidly assembling body of raw recruits—five companies from Decatur County, the Terre Haute Rifles, and later two companies from Lafayette—became the 76th Indiana Infantry Regiment. It was a regiment formed in direct response to Johnson's Newburg raid with orders to hunt down the infamous "hospital robber and his 40 thieves."[29]

Another squadron of soldiers—tolerated out of deference to the commander's unique situation—accompanied the 76th Indiana into Henderson. It was a group of thirty-six volunteers from Warrick County, Indiana, led by none other than Captain Union Bethell. Ironically, they dubbed themselves the "Union Guards of Newburg." After the dreadful fiasco at Newburg, Bethell found himself in an uncomfortable position. In the eyes of many, he had allowed his sacred obligation to slip and was responsible for Newburg's unfortunate, newfound notoriety. The day after the raid, against all reason, people were looking at Union Bethell differently, and he knew it. Bethell, a man whose family name, community stature, and professional business relationships now hung in the balance, was bent on retribution and restoration. Now Bethell was the gambler—double his disgrace or wipe it out.[30]

By the time enough transport was acquired for Morton's new, uncoordinated regiment of Indiana troopers, night had arrived over the muddy Evansville riverbank. The first to take off for Henderson after sunset on July 21 was the steamer *Rob Roy* carrying the mixed command from Columbus, Kentucky. These soldiers would act as the advance guard in the recapture of Henderson, arriving ahead of the main body that would follow on the *Clara Dolson*. The Union ferry service would roil the black waters between Henderson and Evansville all night long until daybreak.[31]

Union Bethell's avengers arrived in Evansville at 9:00 PM, ready for action. Unable to board a steamship that could carry the entire platoon at once, Bethell's men split into two groups. The first set of twenty men equipped with their horses, Springfield rifles, and sidearms were transported across and arrived safely in Henderson sometime after 10:00 PM; the waterfront was now pitch dark. The second shipment of men and materials was brought along by steam ferry *Dime Orphan Boy*. Unfortunately, the heavily loaded transport chose this trip to live up to its name. The ship set out from Evansville just past midnight "when about the middle of the river, the boat was discovered to be sinking. The fact was communicated to those on board by the ferryman, when a scene of wild confusion ensued. Some stripped themselves and others mounted their horses. The horses themselves partook of the panic and commenced striving to get off the boat."[32]

The passing *Eugene* lowered a yawl with a rescue crew, but the small craft was nearly swamped when the tug *Restless* thoughtlessly sped by in the darkness. "In the meanwhile the cries of the men, who had by this time got into the water with their horses, and were struggling for life, became appalling. A flat on the Kentucky side was finally taken to their assistance, and the men were all rescued except one." When roll was taken on the Henderson riverfront, twenty-nine-year-old carpenter and Ohio native George M. Riggs of Boonville did not answer. Standing only five-foot six and loaded down with gear and guns, he had drowned in the darkness and confusion following the boat's demise. In a sad, symbolic denouement, Riggs's horse, borrowed for the mission, had found its way, exhausted, unaided, and riderless, back to its owner miles from the site of the accident.[33]

Because the wet, depleted men had lost all their things, they returned to Evansville, still willing but unarmed. General Love was informed of the accident and arranged for the survivors to be re-equipped and to continue on to Henderson in the company of Lieutenant Colonel Foster. By 8:00 AM on July 22, Bethell's somewhat despondent makeshift cavalrymen were among hundreds of Federal soldiers in the town of Henderson. Weathering the tragic but temporary setback of last evening's transport debacle, Bethell was now ready to set off into the war zone of the Kentucky countryside. He would be on Adam Johnson's home ground.[34]

General Love instructed the 63rd Illinois to station itself at Henderson while the Indiana troops arranged themselves to march toward the interior. Again, Henderson was subject to the dizzying political whipsaw of reoccupation. Over a thousand bluecoats cluttered the red mud banks of the Henderson waterfront, officially returning the citizenry to their battlefield status. Following General Love's orders, Colonel Francis Moro of the 63rd Illinois set himself up as post commander in Henderson. He immediately initiated security measures leading to several arrests. A few of Johnson's men, living in comfort at Henderson since July 17, were also summarily scooped up and hauled off in leg irons.[35]

Later that same day, just as Union troops were taking up positions in Henderson, the *Big Grey Eagle* brought a peculiar cargo downstream to Evansville. The boat docked, and off stepped the entire eighty-five-man collection of convalescent soldiers who had been captured and paroled by Adam Johnson at Newburg. All things considered, it was thought unsafe to keep the defenseless soldiers in Newburg any longer. Of course, the soldiers were quick to relate details to the eager Evansville grapevine. Their recollection was the kind of spin common in political debate. They stated that they "would have defended the town and themselves, if they had been armed." The picture of ill, empty-handed convalescents staring into the barrel of a cocked Rebel weapon was a sympathetic one, but with the Union soldiers equipped with muskets and cartridges in hand, the story was a bit more ambiguous. There was no getting away from the fact that several dozen Federal soldiers had surrendered to one man possessing little more than a dose of bravado and an old shotgun.[36]

CHAPTER 5

Solitude in Slaughtersville

Adam Johnson kept a low public profile in the days directly following the raid, stationing his headquarters on friendly ground in Slaughtersville. Johnson, basking in the rarified glow of what he had accomplished, was now rapidly becoming a folk hero to those of the Southern cause. Union volunteerism wasn't the only thing kick-started by the Newburg raid; Johnson's Breckinridge Guards also experienced a significant jump in numbers, taking in an average of two recruits per day in the weeks following the raid. Johnson's efforts, though laudable for a single person with no recruiting infrastructure, weren't enough. Morton had put more than a thousand soldiers in Henderson in three days; Johnson's band after six weeks of action was now nearing fifty men.[37]

While in hiding, Johnson decided to update General Breckinridge. He made a complete but exaggerated account. Johnson was careful with his events and spent some time piecing together the chronology. He hit all the highlights, beginning with his recruiting failures in early June, the capture of Major Kimbley on June 20, the Henderson barracks attack on June 29, the Madisonville strike on July 5, the capture of Henderson on July 17, and the stunning Newburg raid on July 18. For a man who could not find a single recruit in early June, he had assembled a busy résumé. Despite four dangerous military operations, the Breckinridge Guards had not yet sustained a single combat casualty. It was a distinction that was about to change.[38]

Johnson got word on July 23 that Henderson was mobbed with Federal soldiers, more soldiers than had ever come before. The city administration, friendly to Johnson's visit less than a week ago, was under pressure again. Steamers began to arrive from Evansville returning Henderson refugees who had fled the Confederate takeover. Union sympathizers now felt safe and wasted no time turning the tables on those who had made life difficult for them after the Rebel occupation. Yet again, arrests resumed in earnest.

Adam Johnson was not afraid; being the heavy underdog was the only role he had known his whole life. The odds were no worse for him now than they were only three weeks ago when he had attacked the National Hotel in Henderson with only himself and two others. As always, things would require his special brand of attention. He would harbor his greatest weapon—surprise—and use it only when all the cards were in his favor. Though confident, he had no doubt that Union patrols would be hunting his fledgling company. Johnson adapted. With greater Federal numbers, targets would now be easier to find. Among the hundreds of Union bluecoats now fanned out into the countryside, surely some would get careless.

CHAPTER 6

Union Bethell's Revenge

Early Tuesday morning, July 22, two additional volunteer companies arrived in Evansville. News of the raid had been announced at church services in Lafayette, Indiana, the previous Sunday, after which 225 men stepped forward to join the hunt for "Johnson and his 40 thieves." Leading the Lafayette contingent was Radical Republican Godlove Stein Orth. No time was wasted. Upon arrival, one company boarded the *Courier* and steamed over to the disorder in Henderson. Orth's company joined the *Horner* as makeshift marines and patrolled the Indiana border towns between New Albany and Mount Vernon.[39]

After breakfast in Henderson, a sizable Union detachment organized itself and started for Petersburg. By far the most notorious collection of soldiers on the scene was the casually clothed band of riders from Warrick County, Union Bethell's men. Wherever Bethell went, whispers regarding his capture at Newburg followed. He was intent on reversing his humiliation by taking the hard line. When the regiment finally parted Henderson for the countryside, Bethell's men were in the lead.

All was eventless until early afternoon when two figures were spotted in the distance taking flight. A shot was fired, and the "redshirts" were gone. Who were they? Bethell's men thought they were Adam Johnson and Jack Thompson. The Warrick soldiers made camp for the night nine miles south of Henderson, knee-deep in unknown territory. If it *were* Johnson that the men had come upon that afternoon, where would he be when they slept? Pickets were posted.[40]

At 2:00 AM Wednesday morning, the supply train once again took to the road with Bethell's company in the advance guard. At daybreak, they hit pay dirt. At the house of "the notorious guerrilla chief Willie Fields," Bethell found a cache of twenty muskets, along with several sabers, pistols, and blankets taken from Newburg during the raid. He was on the right track. Fields was chained, interrogated, and then led away to prison.[41]

Before noon on Wednesday, the Union command separated; Bethell's men took the fork toward Slaughtersville while Gavin's regiment went on to Petersburg. Slaughtersville was the town where Johnson had spent much of the last month recruiting and was a well-known hive of Southern sympathy. In fact, the Slaughtersville townsfolk were throwing a big barbecue in celebration of the Newburg raid when word came that Bethell's guardsmen were on the way.[42]

Three of Bethell's advance guard, cautiously cantering their way to Slaughtersville, froze when a mounted local toting a drawn double-barreled shotgun appeared and commanded them to halt. With Bethell's "dirty little command" dressed in the familiar clothes of country farmers, the armed stranger approached, thinking himself about to meet some fresh Confederate recruits. In a moment, the remaining Warrick riders came up and surrounded the man now recognized as John Patterson. Patterson, dressed in Confederate gray trousers, a yellow shirt, and a black felt hat with the Stars and Bars, was one of the Newburg raiders and the Rebel who personally had plundered Bethell's home. According to Johnson, he was one of his bravest men. Now trapped, Patterson gripped his newly acquired pistols and started firing in an attempt to blast his way free of the Federal circle. After he emptied his weapons without effect, the smoke cleared to reveal Bethell's cavalry figuratively closing the noose. A dismounted soldier grabbed Patterson's horse bridle, momentarily ending the excitement. John Patterson, a man who claimed that his pursuers would have to "cut every tree and burn every bush in three counties" to find him, surrendered. Without introduction, one of Bethell's riders, Dr. McGill, rode up to the captive, put his gun to Patterson's head, and pulled the trigger. A single, shattering, smoke-filled concussion echoed out across the hills. The Rebel dropped from his horse and fell lifeless to the dust. Initially, he was thought to be dead. Instead, he precariously stood up to reveal both eyes blown from their sockets and a face and front covered in blood. The bullet had passed through both eye sockets, taking away part of his nose, but had not pene-trated his brain. Staggering perhaps a hundred yards and watched curiously by the Federal onlookers, he finally fell while begging for his life. Bethell's men briefly questioned the badly wounded Confederate and then left him writhing piteously alone on the roadside.[43]

But John Patterson would not die. He was picked up by friends and brought to a nearby farmhouse where he was treated for his wounds. Owen and Johnson came to visit him, and in time he would be healed. The grim horrors of war could come to both sides.[44]

CHAPTER 7

Rural Encounters

On Thursday afternoon, July 24, Colonel James Gavin, field commander of the 76th Indiana Infantry Regiment, got careless in enemy territory with deadly consequences. With summer temperatures above ninety degrees and a linen coat covering his rank, Gavin led a small rickety wagon train out onto the desolate, dust-covered road from Petersburg back to Henderson. After two days in the field, the haphazardly organized regiment was in need of supplies, and Gavin decided to lead the one-day road trip back to base. Because nothing much had been encountered by Gavin's men on the outbound journey just two days before, the rolling Kentucky hillsides were presumed secure. They were not. Colonel Gavin, Dr. Horace Wirtz, First Lieutenant John H. Braden, and Private Deloss Thompson were cantering northward at about 3:00 PM when they were ambushed by Confederate partisans.[45]

Alerted by the oncoming dust cloud rising from the hoof beats in the distance, Lorenzo Dow Fisher, a small, wiry, long-haired figure under Adam Johnson's Confederate command, collected about a dozen countrymen and prepared for battle. "Rens" Fisher carefully positioned his men in the roadside brush near an old, straight half-mile racetrack where locals occasionally gathered to match horses and down drinks. With shotguns loaded, the tension building as minutes stretched out in the oppressive heat, the Rebels abruptly unleashed a shower of deadly buckshot on the stunned Union riders. Colonel Gavin suffered a shotgun ball that passed entirely through his hand, Dr. Wirtz received a ball that lodged painfully in his shoulder, and Lieutenant Braden was severely wounded. The startled horses, also all wounded, lit out down the road with their riders away from the ambush.[46]

After riding a few steps, Lieutenant Braden slipped from his saddle and fell to the road in a heap, throwing up a small cloud of dust with the impact. The lieutenant had been struck with a mass of six or seven balls in the upper body and had been literally "shot to pieces." Braden, a native of Greensburg, was the only officer from the 76th Indiana killed in combat during its term of service.[47]

Colonel Gavin and the others acknowledged Braden's fall, but they didn't stop. They suspected they'd be followed, and they weren't wrong. A mile down the road, with wounded horses finally quitting, the three dismounted and plunged into a roadside cornfield. The Confederate band tracked them down. Quiet as field mice, the three Union soldiers didn't move a muscle as the enemy trod the field around them, coming within yards at one point during the search. The only sounds in their ears were their own heartbeats; the only movement was the hot surge of blood in their arteries. Fisher's men, unaware they had cornered a Union regimental commander, gave up the search as darkness crept over the landscape.[48]

In the black of the July night, Gavin, Wirtz, and Thompson emerged from the green cornstalks and slowly wandered the roads northward. The bedraggled nomads knocked on doors along the way seeking directions to Henderson. The exhausted, dehydrated, dirt-covered—and, for Gavin and Wirtz, bloody—men arrived at a Henderson outpost after daybreak. They were taken to headquarters where they were treated for their wounds. Only Private Thompson escaped unharmed. Within hours, news of the attack was broadcast throughout Henderson and Evansville. Indignation reigned once again.[49]

Union intelligence in the wake of the Gavin attack was intensified, and a report was received that two well-known Confederate regulars attended church services every Sunday at Pleasant Valley, southeast of Henderson. On the solemn Sunday morning of July 27, "Rens" Fisher and his good friend "Tennessee" George stepped outside the Pleasant Valley Meeting House after church and promptly found themselves engulfed in a swirling hail of bullets. Suddenly the tables were turned, as Fisher and George found themselves on the receiving end of an enemy ambush. The Yankee squadron kept a heated fire on the two Confederates, at one point even shooting toward the innocent crowd milling around after services. The men ran for their horses while Federal bullets pockmarked the side of the old log church. The Rebels got away unharmed.[50]

The gangly, thin Fisher—a veteran of Johnson's Henderson takeover, a likely member of the Newburg Raiders, and eventual captain of Johnson's Partisan Rangers, Company B—was tracked down outside his father's house and killed by a Federal bullet before the year was out.[51]

CHAPTER 8

Redemption Declared

On July 25, 1862, the *Daily Evansville Journal* carried the following bold and somewhat misleading headline:

GOOD NEWS FROM KENTUCKY!

GUERRILLAS ROUTED BY

CAPTAIN BETHEL

MOST OF THE GUNS STOLEN AT

NEWBURG RECOVERED

Union Bethell had been out in the Kentucky wild for several days, and his attitude remained intense. His Warrick County posse had enlisted for ten days, and already time was running out. After leaving Newburg in haste, Bethell's improvised cavalry experienced the usual hardships of army life. They possessed few tents and subsisted on a shoestring diet of pork, bread, and coffee, but the only thing Bethell acknowledged was the business of hunting his foes. After the confrontation with Patterson, Johnson's Breckinridge Guards knew their Newburg opponent was near. Bethell had taken "ten prisoners, two flags, and ten or twelve horses" in addition to the recaptured Newburg weapons.[52]

Bethell and his men returned to Henderson on July 25 to drop off prisoners, and on July 27 they were back pursuing the enemy on the Henderson–Madisonville Road. For the next several days, Bethell's vigilantes camped near Green River, the clock rapidly ticking down on his men and their commitment. With his ten-day term ending, Bethell called for seventy more Warrick volunteers to continue his zealous pursuit. Time, however, had cooled the heat generated by the Newburg attack, and no further independent expedition was mounted by Bethell or Warrick County.[53]

With the same vexing habit displayed by outnumbered civilian combatants ages over, Johnson's minutemen melted back to the innocence of the plow, awaiting once again the season to emerge.[54]

CHAPTER 9

Foster's Command

For several days an article had circulated in the *Daily Evansville Journal* addressed to the men of the 25th Indiana. All soldiers from the 25th Indiana, whether convalescing or visiting, were required to assemble for duty on July 26. A steamer was scheduled to take them to Memphis to rejoin the regiment. Colonel Foster was headed back to his unit. At least, that was his intention.[55]

Lt. Colonel John Watson Foster
Reprinted from *Indiana at Shiloh*

The unanticipated wounding of Colonel Gavin and the desire of military authorities in Cairo to return the 63rd Illinois left General Love in a bind. He needed a competent officer to take command at Henderson, and Foster's willing help during the recent emergency was impressive. Barely hours before Foster was to board a steamer for Tennessee, General Love approached him to serve in western Kentucky. Foster accepted, and the announcement was made. Governor Morton would see to the transfer.[56]

Love quickly reorganized his command. On Saturday evening, July 26, General Love, Lieutenant Colonel Foster, and a small entourage that included a correspondent from the *Daily Evansville Journal* set out to Henderson. Once in town, Love's group proceeded to Union headquarters at the Hancock House, where all of the officers who had served in the

Henderson invasion were gathered. Gratitude was offered to Colonel Moro and Legion Captain Bethell, and Foster was welcomed to his new command by Mayor Hall. Colonel Gavin, having lost his sword during the ambush earlier in the week, was ceremoniously presented with a brand new saber. Amid the smiles and speeches, Love was satisfied that a smooth transfer of power had taken place. It was the dawn of a new era in Henderson. It was now Colonel Foster's responsibility to guarantee security after the recent upheavals. He would govern with an iron fist for the following year.[57]

On July 26, the official order came through concerning the legitimacy of the Johnson paroles given out at Newburg. Brigadier General Boyle issued a proclamation stating that the paroles were "to be regarded as an oath administered by any other robber, and considered in no other way." Not surprisingly, given the status of Johnson's men at the time, the paroles were never recognized nor registered with either of the warring governments. It's likely that Johnson understood that his paroles carried no weight from the start. It may have been his final trick in the Confederate raid on Newburg, Indiana.[58]

Epilogue

In the months ahead, Colonel Foster would institute an uncompromising regime in Henderson. The problem for citizens was no longer too few Union soldiers but rather too many. The large Federal contingent did not stand on etiquette; if they needed anything—from wood for an evening fire to whiskey or even cash money—they often just took it. With more than a thousand soldiers permanently stationed in northwest Kentucky, little Henderson came under a destructive siege. Cattle, horses, wagons—whatever was necessary to keep a poorly supplied army in operation—were procured from the locals. Foster became a hated symbol of the unjustified depredations wrought on a vulnerable citizenry.[59]

General Boyle inflamed the contentious political opposition by issuing his famous Order No. 5:

"No person hostile in opinion to the Government and desiring its overthrow will be allowed to stand for office in the District of Kentucky. The attempt of such a person to stand for office will be regarded as in itself sufficient evidence of his treasonable intent to warrant arrest...."[60]

Foster had no problem with Boyle's order and came down like a hammer on the political establishment. The Federal commander forced the Henderson city council to take an oath of loyalty to the Union cause. Anyone who would not comply would be removed from office. The council refused the oath and resigned *en masse*. It was a "no-lose" situation for Foster as Union supporters replaced them. Mayor Hall, on the other hand, left his post in August and became a member of Johnson's band. In November, Hall would mimic Johnson's achievement by crossing the Ohio River with a small Confederate force to raid West Franklin, Indiana, for guns and horses.[61]

On August 20, the short-lived 76th Indiana came to the end of its thirty-day service term. The 65th Indiana Infantry, a regiment formed in

Princeton, Indiana, in response to Lincoln's July call, replaced it. Foster was promoted to regimental commander of the 65th and remained in the Henderson environs for nearly a year. By mid-1863, the Henderson County Courthouse had a new name—"Foster's military prison."[62]

Before the raid there were at least four missed opportunities for Newburg Legion troops to come to attention: after the headline reports of Johnson's Henderson attack in June; when General Love ordered his regional Legion commander, General James Blythe, to communicate with Newburg about readiness after July 5; when a Warrick County inspection scheduled by General Love was pre-empted on July 12; and when newspaper reports of Morgan's "First Kentucky Raid" rattled the Bluegrass during the second week of July. Indeed, many Newburg townsfolk initially thought Johnson *was* Morgan when Johnson arrived in town on July 18. Combine these events with the rumor of underground Rebel activity in southern Indiana and known disaffection in Newburg, and one might well have considered the deck stacked firmly against a successful raid. Unfortunately for Newburg, luck and human complacency conspired against a sincere appraisal of the possibilities.

The arrests of the Newburg residents who allegedly aided the enemy raiders led to some surprising legal outcomes. Dr. Tilman, blamed for surrendering the soldiers in the Exchange Hotel without a fight, was "honorably discharged" four days after his arrest. With sick soldiers holding unloaded muskets and Tilman's service record supporting his credentials, it was clear the Newburg Hospital director did the best he could; there just hadn't been enough time to defend the town. It's likely that Governor Morton interrogated Tilman, as the order releasing him was issued the same day Morton left Evansville. No one else possessed the authority to render such a summary decision.[63]

In November 1862, Andrew Huston, allegedly the Rebels' most overt assistant on the day of the Newburg raid, was tried in Indianapolis for treason. The jury deadlocked on a vote of eight for conviction and four for acquittal. The prosecution angrily retried Huston in May of 1863, only to be greeted by a unanimous verdict for acquittal. With its best case down the drain, the state had no alternative but to release the remaining prisoners. Were the arrested Newburg citizens unjustly accused? Was it possible the *Daily Evansville Journal* and the hysterical Newburg citizenry misinterpreted the events of July 18, 1862? Was Huston actually "pressed into service" the day of the raid as suggested by E. L. Starling decades later? As hinted by Solomon Coker while in an Indianapolis prison in December 1862, perhaps people were just too scared to speak up for those known to be innocent.[64]

As for Adam "Stovepipe" Johnson, the aftermath of the summer of 1862 led to the formation of the 10th Confederate Kentucky Cavalry Regiment, known later as the "Partisan Rangers." The Rangers would continue to surprise Union garrisons in Kentucky and Tennessee through the end of 1862 and into 1863. In the summer of 1863, the Partisan Rangers reluctantly joined General John Hunt Morgan's "Great Raid" into Indiana and Ohio. Johnson and Morgan struck a deal that allowed Johnson to participate in the raid up to the point of the Ohio River crossing. He would then be detached by steamer and would move west against towns on the lower Ohio, including Henderson and Evansville. At the last minute, Morgan reneged and burned the steamer without Johnson's knowledge. The Great Raid, although spectacular in concept, ended in disaster. The 10th Confederate Kentucky Cavalry, a regiment carefully built by the relentless vision of one man, was hunted down and destroyed. The famous "Stovepipe" Johnson was reduced to swimming the Ohio River to elude Federal clutches. General Morgan and most of his command were captured and thrown in prison.[65]

For a year following the summer of 1862, Henderson remained in firm Union control. Johnson's Newburg raid provided fresh evidence to a lethargic Indiana Legion that it was time to confront the dangers of Confederates in Kentucky. The 76th, 65th, and 78th Indiana regiments were fueled, in part, by the indignation felt by Hoosier patriots in the wake of the raid on Indiana. But the story, like the war, would not end in 1863.

In 1864, with Kentucky once again firmly behind Union battle lines in the deep South, Newburg and Henderson returned as the focus of Confederate intrigue. Reprising his appearance on the scene would be none other than Adam "Stovepipe" Johnson. Johnson, now a Brigadier General attempting to rebuild Southern units in Kentucky, received a communication from the Northern secret societies that had popped up in opposition to emancipation in Illinois, Indiana, and Ohio. In August, more than ten thousand Southern sympathizers from these three states were to rendezvous at Newburg, Indiana, in what has come to be known as the Northwest Conspiracy. Commandeered steamers from Green River would transport Johnson's Confederate regulars across to Indiana. His men would then link up with the traitorous forces collected at Newburg and subject southern Indiana to Confederate control. The plan would come to full fruition with the capture of Evansville, the rails bringing further allies from Indianapolis, Chicago, and beyond. Like so much of the Southern cause in the late war years, the plan was more a pale, faded fancy than anything that could ever come true. On August 21, General Adam Johnson, at the head of a column of captured Union soldiers at Grubbs Crossing, Kentucky, was struck in the face by a musket ball fired in error by his own men, blinding him and ending his military career and nearly his life. He became a Federal prisoner.[66]

APPENDIX

When I wrote this book it was my desire to maintain a certain pace to the work. To do so meant there was a limit to the number of characters and the depth of detail that could be offered in the main story. Therefore, for those who may want more, I have added several special sections at the end of this volume that may serve further interest in the subject.

Cast of Characters
In Alphabetical Order

Barrett, John—Wealthy uncle and former employer of the adolescent Adam Rankin Johnson. Barrett serves as Johnson's safe harbor in Henderson, Kentucky, during the war.

Bethell, Thomas—Former Indiana State Militia colonel, former Mexican War company captain, and wealthy Newburg businessman. He is the Bethell family patriarch and older brother to Union Bethell.

Bethell, Union—Wealthy captain of the Newburg Home Guard company the day of the Confederate raid. He is the younger brother of Thomas Bethell.

Blythe, James—General and commander of Indiana Legion (Home Guard) forces on Indiana's Ohio River border.

Boyle, Jeremiah—U.S. general and commander of all Union garrison forces in Kentucky from mid-1862 to 1864.

Braden, John—Lieutenant of the 76th Indiana Infantry. He is ambushed and killed by a squadron of Adam Johnson's commandos led by Lorenzo Dow Fisher.

Breckinridge, John—Confederate general who gives Adam Johnson and Robert Martin verbal orders to raise a regiment of Confederate soldiers in Federal-held Kentucky.

Carney, Henry Hampton "Hamp"—Newburg wharfmaster and one of the conspirators to seek out Adam Johnson about an attack on the Newburg armory.

Daly, John—Captain of the Louisville Provost Guard, Company E. He is wounded in Adam Johnson's Henderson attack of June 29 and leaves Henderson for Louisville.

Darby, John—Former captain of Company H, 25th Indiana Infantry Regiment. Darby retires from service in April 1862 and returns to Newburg in time to witness the Confederate raid on July 18.

Dexter, Henry—Steamboat captain based in Evansville, Indiana. He throws a big Fourth of July party on the *Courier* and later pilots the same steamboat on the afternoon of the raid in an attempt to cut off the escaping raiders.

Dixon, Archibald—Former lieutenant governor of Kentucky and prominent citizen of Henderson. He tries to find common ground between the fractious political elements in town after Johnson's Henderson attack of June 29. He later is part of a delegation charged with getting Adam Johnson and his troops to leave Henderson on July 17, 1862.

Fisher, Lorenzo—A member of Adam Johnson's Breckinridge Guards and likely member of the Newburg raiders. Fisher's squad later ambushes the party of Colonel James Gavin and kills Lieutenant John Braden of the 76th Indiana Infantry. A few days later, Fisher himself is ambushed and nearly killed by a Union patrol.

Foster, John Watson—Union lieutenant colonel called upon to assemble the response after Evansville learned about the Newburg raid on the afternoon of July 18, 1862. Foster's help eventually lands him the position of commander of Union forces in Henderson, Kentucky. Later, he receives regimental command of the 65th Indiana Infantry.

Gavin, James—Colonel and primary recruiter of the 76th Indiana Infantry. He and a group of three Union soldiers are ambushed when they become careless riding back to Henderson from the Kentucky countryside. Gavin is wounded in the hand and nearly captured.

George, "Tennessee" Julius—A member of Adam Johnson's Breckinridge Guards. He helps Johnson's escape plan after the Newburg raid and later is nearly killed by a Union patrol.

Hale, Luther—First lieutenant and commander of a detachment from the 1st Michigan Light Artillery Regiment, Battery F, Andrews's Battery. The small group from Andrews's Battery garrisons Henderson, Kentucky, for three weeks and is subject to attack, depression, and near disintegration during their stay.

Hall, Edwin—Mayor of Henderson, Kentucky. Hall eventually abandons his post as mayor and joins Adam Johnson's Confederate troopers.

Hatchett, George—Niagara, Kentucky, citizen who harbors Adam Johnson after the June Henderson attack on the Union barracks.

Henry, Sergeant—Union soldier who belatedly accepts command of the convalescent Federal troops at the Exchange Hotel hospital on the day of Johnson's raid on Newburg.

Johnson, Adam "Stovepipe"—Confederate officer and the main character of the story.

Kimbley, John—Union major and regimental surgeon who becomes Adam Johnson's first captive.

Love, John—General and commander of all Indiana State Legion (Home Guard) forces.

Martin, Robert—Scout for Lieutenant Colonel Nathan Bedford Forrest. Martin is part of Johnson's operations in Kentucky, a member of the Newburg raiders, and works with Johnson to form and officer the Partisan Rangers.

Mefford, Elliott—Conspirator who finds Adam Johnson and tells him about the idle armory in Newburg.

Morgan, John Hunt—Confederate cavalry colonel (or acting brigadier general) who embarks on a raid through the center of Kentucky during July 1862.

Moro, Francis—Colonel of the 63rd Illinois Infantry Regiment and garrison commander of Henderson, Kentucky, for several days after the Newburg raid.

Morton, Oliver—Governor of Indiana.

Nicklin, Benjamin—No-nonsense captain of the 13th Indiana Light Artillery Regiment, Nicklin's Battery. Nicklin's men help garrison Henderson for about eleven days in early July.

Patterson, John—Sebree, Kentucky, native and early member of Johnson's Breckinridge Guards. He is the Newburg raider who plunders the Home Guard captain's house and who later is cornered and shot by Union Bethell's posse in Kentucky.

Perkins, Charles—Union gunboat commander who eventually ejects Adam Johnson's cavalry company from Henderson on July 17, 1862.

Smith, Green Clay—Union general who takes command of the Federal garrison at Henderson, Kentucky, for four days in mid-July 1862.

Soaper, William—Wealthy tobacco grower who plays unexpected host to Adam Johnson's cavalry company on the night of July 17, 1862.

Strong, William—Union general and New York Abolitionist who commands U.S. Army units in the District of Cairo, Illinois.

Tilman, John—Doctor and veteran of the 60th Indiana Infantry Regiment who has unofficial charge of the convalescent Federal soldiers on the day of the Newburg raid. He is later arrested, but quickly released, for his part in the raid.

Topping, Melville—Captain of the Union Rifles of Terre Haute, an independent Union infantry company. They were one of the first groups to respond to Governor Morton's call for volunteers to quell Rebels in northwestern Kentucky after the Newburg raid.

Tyler, George—Second lieutenant and second in command of the 1st Michigan Light Artillery Regiment, Battery F detachment in Henderson. He is later killed in a night attack on the Henderson barracks at the end of June 1862.

Event Timeline
1862

Friday, June 20	Confederate irregulars raid the Calhoun, Kentucky, Courthouse.
	U.S. Major John F. Kimbley, surgeon 11th U.S. Kentucky, is captured by the Breckinridge Guards.
	Newspaper reports of smallpox in Henderson, Kentucky.
Sunday, June 22	A fifty-man detachment from Andrews's Battery arrives in Henderson, Kentucky.
Monday, June 23	Steamer *Golden State* arrives at Evansville from the Tennessee River, bringing a large quantity of sick and wounded Indiana soldiers to hospitals in Evansville, Indiana.
Wednesday, June 25	Louisville Provost Guard, Company E, arrives in Henderson.
	Steamer *Stephen Decatur* arrives at Evansville from the Tennessee River, bringing a large quantity of sick and wounded Indiana soldiers to hospitals in Evansville.
Saturday, June 28	Adam Johnson learns of Union troops in Henderson and decides to attack.
	Union soldiers begin arresting Southern sympathizers in Henderson.
Sunday, June 29	The wife and four children of General U.S. Grant overnight in Evansville.
	Attack on the National Hotel in Henderson by the Breckinridge Guards "Band of Three."

Monday, June 30   Citizens' meeting is held in Henderson and a resolution is drafted condemning the National attack.

Johnson's Breckinridge Guards hide out for the next few days in Niagara, Kentucky.

Tuesday, July 1   Lincoln calls on the loyal States for 300,000 three-year volunteers.

Nicklin's Battery arrives in Henderson.

Steamer *Lancaster No. 4* arrives at Evansville from the Tennessee River, bringing a large quantity of sick and wounded Ohio soldiers to hospitals in Evansville.

A severe heat wave descends on the region; temperatures near 90 degrees for the next two weeks.

Wednesday, July 2   Union Lieutenant Colonel John Watson Foster arrives in Evansville to bury his dead brother-in-law, Lieutenant Alexander McFerson.

Friday, July 4   Independence Day celebrations take place throughout Indiana and Kentucky.

Dexter's party on the *Courier.*

Johnson learns of Union cavalry at Madisonville, Kentucky, and decides to attack.

Confederate Colonel (Acting Brigadier General) John Hunt Morgan moves to begin his summer raid on central Kentucky.

Saturday, July 5	Seven civilians (Southern sympathizers) from Henderson are sent to Louisville for imprisonment.
	Bandits are reported robbing citizens outside Henderson.
	Attack on the 1st and 2nd Battalions of the 9th Pennsylvania Cavalry in Madisonville by the Breckinridge Guards "Band of Six."
Sunday, July 6	Johnson returns to Henderson and drafts his response to the resolutions published in the *Henderson Weekly Reporter* of July 3, 1862.
Monday, July 7	Indiana Governor Oliver Morton announces the particulars of the eleven regiments required by Indiana to satisfy Lincoln's quota for three-year volunteers.
	Steamer *D. A. January* arrives at Evansville, bringing a large quantity of sick and wounded Indiana soldiers to hospitals in Evansville.
	Major General John Love, commander of all Indiana Legion forces, arrives in Evansville to review preparedness throughout southern Indiana.
Tuesday, July 8	65th Indiana Infantry begins to assemble in Princeton, Indiana.
	Recruitment efforts begin across Indiana in order to meet the Lincoln volunteer quotas.
	General Love tours Evansville Home Guard units.
Wednesday, July 9	General Love tours Mount Vernon, Indiana, Home Guard units.
	Morgan's Raiders capture Tompkinsville, Kentucky, and defeat the 3rd Battalion, 9th Pennsylvania Cavalry.

Thursday, July 10

Large recruitment gathering is held at Evansville. Speeches are given by General Love, Captain Nicklin, General James E. Blythe, and several local Indiana Legion company commanders.

General Green Clay Smith arrives at Henderson as the new ranking officer and Henderson post commander.

A typical cycle of Midwest summer thunderstorms begins.

Morgan's Raiders capture Glasgow, Kentucky.

Friday, July 11

Morgan's Raiders capture Lebanon, Kentucky.

Saturday, July 12

Nicklin's Battery leaves Henderson for Louisville to defend against Morgan's raid into central Kentucky.

Many guerrilla attacks are reported throughout western Kentucky.

Governor Morton orders General Love to stop his activities in southern Indiana and to proceed to Louisville to meet with General Boyle about Morgan's raid.

Morgan's Raiders capture Springfield and Mackville, Kentucky.

Sunday, July 13

General Love meets with General Boyle in Louisville.

Morgan's Raiders capture Harrodsburg, Kentucky.

Monday, July 14	A severe thunderstorm knocks out telegraph service in Evansville.
	General Love leaves Louisville and arrives in New Albany, Indiana, to continue his organization of local Home Guard units in southern Indiana.
	General G. Clay Smith, Andrews's Battery, and the Louisville Provost Guard troops leave Henderson for Louisville to defend against Morgan's raid into central Kentucky.
	1st and 2nd Battalions of the 9th Pennsylvania Cavalry arrive in Henderson from Madisonville, Kentucky.
	Morgan's Raiders capture Laurenceburg, Kentucky.
Tuesday, July 15	9th Pennsylvania Cavalry leaves Henderson for Louisville to defend against Morgan's raid into central Kentucky.
	A final Henderson shipment of prisoners—Southern Rights sympathizers—is sent to Louisville.
	Morgan's Raiders capture Georgetown, Kentucky.
Wednesday, July 16	Henderson is an open city. Union sympathizers and hospitalized Union soldiers begin evacuating to Evansville.
	Lightning storms continue to interrupt telegraph service to Evansville.
	Johnson meets with John Barrett and learns of the Henderson evacuation. Johnson decides to capture Henderson the next day.

Thursday, July 17   Johnson's Breckinridge Guards capture Henderson unopposed. Later, most of Johnson's men retreat to the William Soaper farm.

Johnson confers with Elliott Mefford, Andrew Mefford, and Hamp Carney from Newburg, Indiana, about the possibility of capturing the arms held in a riverside warehouse in Newburg.

Telegraph service to Evansville remains unavailable.

Traffic on the lower Ohio River comes to a stop in reaction to Johnson's possession of Henderson.

Morgan's Raiders capture Cynthiana, Kentucky, after a difficult fight.

Friday, July 18   Johnson's Breckinridge Guards capture Newburg, Indiana, stealing weapons and looting the town.

The Evansville rescue mission to Newburg is too late to capture the fleeing Breckinridge Guards.

Telegraph service is restored to Evansville by late afternoon.

Indiana Governor Morton is notified of the attack on Indiana soil.

Ram steamer *T. D. Horner* arrives in Evansville.

Some soldiers from Johnson's troop remain in Henderson, essentially controlling the town.

Morgan's Raiders capture Paris, Kentucky.

Saturday, July 19	Governor Morton begins a statewide mobilization to thwart Johnson's Breckinridge Guards.
	Colonels Gavin and Wilder obtain five hundred recruits from Decatur County, Indiana, in four hours' time.
	General Love arrives back in Evansville and takes charge of troops assembling to invade Henderson.
	Union Rifles of Terre Haute arrive in Evansville.
	Troops and steamers from Cairo, Illinois, head for Evansville to aid in the operation to recapture Henderson.
Sunday, July 20	Rumors abound regarding further Confederate attacks on Indiana—none of them are true, yet.
	Morgan's Raiders capture Richmond, Kentucky.
Monday, July 21	Governor Morton arrives in Evansville. He gives speeches and interviews the Newburg citizens arrested after Johnson's raid.
	During the day, troops begin arriving in Evansville from Greensburg and Terre Haute, Indiana, and will eventually be designated the 76th Indiana Infantry. General Love is operations commander for the recapture of Henderson, and Colonel Gavin is field commander of the 76th Indiana.
	After dark, troops begin leaving Evansville for Henderson.
	Henderson is recaptured, and several of Johnson's soldiers are arrested.
	Morgan's Raiders capture Crab Orchard, Kentucky.

Tuesday, July 22

More than a thousand Union troops fan out into the surrounding Henderson County countryside, looking for Johnson's men.

The 63rd Illinois Infantry is ordered to secure the city of Henderson.

Home Guard activities in Evansville are rejuvenated.

Governor Morton returns to Indianapolis.

Dr. Tilman, arrested for allowing the capture of convalescent soldiers at Newburg, is released without charges.

Soldiers from the Newburg Hospital are evacuated to Evansville.

Two hundred twenty-five volunteers from Lafayette, Indiana, arrive in Evansville and join operations in the Henderson–Evansville area.

Morgan's Raiders capture Somerset, Kentucky, and then return to Tennessee.

Wednesday, July 23

Captain Union Bethell, Newburg Home Guard commander, recaptures a small quantity of arms and supplies taken from Newburg by Johnson's raiders.

Evansville telegraph service is again interrupted.

Henderson refugees in Evansville begin returning home.

Union Bethell's men capture and shoot one of Johnson's soldiers, John Patterson.

Thursday, July 24

A group led by one of Johnson's men, Lorenzo Fisher, ambushes a party of Union soldiers led by Colonel James Gavin, wounding two and killing one soldier; Gavin narrowly escapes capture.

Friday, July 25	General Love taps Lt. Colonel John Foster to be the new military post commander at Henderson.
Saturday, July 26	Foster is installed as post commander in Henderson; he will remain in that job for almost a year.
	Guerrilla activity in Henderson County begins to dissipate in the face of Union force in the area.
	Paroles issued by Adam Johnson to the Newburg soldiers are voided.
Sunday, July 27	A Union squadron ambushes two of Johnson's men as they emerge from church; they escape unharmed.

Conspiracy: Elliott Mefford, Andrew Mefford, and Hamp Carney

Elliott Mefford and Hamp Carney are perhaps the most important figures in the Newburg raid; without them it is unlikely that Adam Johnson could have obtained the type of intelligence that would have made Newburg a target. These two men gave the ready predator his prey on a plate.

◆

Elliott Mefford

For this work, Elliott Mefford's age, background, and primary occupation were taken from the *Warrick County, Indiana, 1850 Federal Census*; the *Warrick County, Indiana, 1860 Federal Census*; Goodspeed Brothers' *History of Warrick, Spencer, and Perry Counties*; and several other minor sources.

In the 1850 census, Elliott Mefford is listed as a forty-three-year-old farmer living in Boon Township, Warrick County. It is clear he was not living in the city of Boonville at the time because those listings are specifically sub-headed. He and his forty-three-year-old wife, Mary (Clutter Stevens) Mefford, are listed as Kentucky natives; they were married on March 29, 1842. By the 1850 census, their oldest son, Andrew, is already listed as eight years old. Andrew; his four-year-old sister, Mary; and his three-year-old younger brother, Taylor, were all born in Indiana, indicating the Meffords had been state residents continuously since marriage. Elliott Mefford fought under the command of Thomas Bethell in Company I, 16th U.S. Infantry Regiment during the Mexican War, 1847–1848. In a town as small as Newburg, this service made him a respected man and allowed him to know and perhaps become associated with the Bethell family.

By 1860, the Meffords had moved to Ohio Township, Newburg, and Elliott's occupation is now listed as "trader-farmer." This specific wording is unusual, and he is the only citizen listed like this in Ohio Township. The wording could suggest that trading had become at least as big or perhaps even a bigger part of his occupation compared to farming.

In Lewis's *Newburgh, Indiana; A History of Schools and Families, 1803–1959*, an 1859 list of professions and occupations on page 19 finds Mefford and Stout listed as dealers in drugs and medicines. Because the Elliott Mefford family is the only Mefford family in the 1860 census, it is likely that this druggist partnership was partly owned by Elliott Mefford and was still an ongoing business just before the Civil War. It wouldn't be difficult to see Elliott Mefford as a man traveling both sides of the Ohio River and trading farm produce for potions, poultices, and other stock for his druggist business in Newburg. His Kentucky roots were fed by frequent visits across the river to his home state, where he made contacts, perhaps met family, and engaged in business dealings with like-minded friends. It's probable that nearby Scuffletown and Henderson were his most common Kentucky stops.

◆

Andrew J. Mefford

The *Report of the Adjutant General of the State of Kentucky, Confederate Kentucky Volunteers* was compiled and published some fifty years after the end of the Civil War. As might be expected from the more loosely kept records of Confederate units in Kentucky, it is riddled with demonstrable errors. One, in my view, is the enlistment date for Andrew Mefford. Volume II of the *Kentucky Adjutant General's Report* lists Andrew J. Mefford as joining Johnson on July 1, 1862. This date seems impossible and is likely a convenient compromise due to poor record keeping in the early phases of Johnson's Breckinridge Guards. Johnson's recruitment accelerates after the Union barracks attack at Henderson on June 29. July 1 would be the absolute earliest an Indiana citizen would even know about Johnson's presence from the *Daily Evansville Journal* or other local papers. Andrew Mefford is not listed by Johnson as one of the attackers on the July 5 Madisonville raid. As an Indiana native, it is unlikely that he was one of those sent recruiting in Kentucky prior to that date as mentioned by Johnson in *Partisan Rangers*, page 100.

I have always assumed that Elliott Mefford and his son traveled together on their journey to Henderson on July 17 to find Adam Johnson's Breckinridge Guards. I have no information to support this other than intuition. It is natural for a son to form political opinions at the foot of his parents. To me, it does not seem strange that two accordant men, father and son, would find their way together to give voice to deep-seated beliefs in perhaps the most important moment in the life of each.

The date on which Elliott Mefford first communicated his Newburg scheme to Johnson appears to be unequivocal, if one accepts Johnson's statement in *Partisan Rangers*, page 104,

> "While camped at the Soaper Farm, where there was a cross-road leading toward Newburg, on the opposite bank of the Ohio, I was

informed that there were hundreds of stands of guns in the arsenal of this town."

From this reading it is clear that Elliott Mefford, possibly joined by his son, and certainly by Hamp Carney, met with Adam Johnson for the first time on the evening of July 17, or perhaps in the very early morning hours of July 18, 1862.

Andrew Mefford was promoted to corporal on December 17, 1862, and then captured at the ill-starred conclusion of Morgan's Great Raid on July 20, 1863. He spent time both at Camp Chase and Camp Douglas during the next year. He died December 17, 1864, of pneumonia while in captivity in Chicago.

Henry Hampton "Hamp" Carney II

The second American generation of the Carney family came down the Ohio River from Gallipolis, Ohio, in 1831 and settled on a spot known as the Layne Farm in Vanderburgh County, Indiana. While in southern Indiana, John and Malvina Carney had nine children, six sons and three daughters. Their oldest child, born in 1833, was named Henry Hampton Carney II.

By 1850, the Carney family had moved to Warrick County. Although Hamp's parents, brothers, and sisters are listed as living together as a family in Warrick census records, Henry Hampton is not with them. It's possible that he was already on his own by the age of seventeen. The 1860 Warrick census lists the H. H. Carney family as living in Ohio Township, Newburg, Indiana. Carney is listed as an Indiana native, and his wife is from Ohio. Their two children, a two-year-old girl and an unnamed boy only two months old, are both Indiana natives. "Hamp" Carney was twenty-seven years old in 1860.

Much is made of Carney's listed occupation in conjunction with the events of the raid. Carney was part owner, with L. J. Wakeland, of the Newburg wharfboat. His occupation is listed as "wharfmaster," and he was a forwarding and commissioning agent for goods cycling through Newburg. There is only one other wharfmaster listed in the Ohio Township census of 1860, and no secondary occupation is listed for Carney. Day in and day out, Carney was master of the vital economic link with the river. He knew boat schedules, the river fleet, its captains, and the goods—both legal and illegal—shipped on the river. He was well acquainted with the rhythms of the brown waters of the Ohio. Carney also was well aware of how the town reacted to shipments and who was receiving what. It's probable that he knew the contents of each and every warehouse in town, including the Bethell warehouse where the idle guns were stored.

Carney likely came to know Elliott Mefford as a result of Mefford's budding occupation as a trader on the river. No doubt the two of them had time to talk on the Newburg wharf about conditions in Kentucky and about the impact the war was having on their businesses. The war had made things difficult for both of them, dramatically decreasing the prospects for the free flow of goods on the river. By early 1862, Newburg's association with the river had turned into a liability. The absence of the railroad and the ravages of war had delivered a sad message to Newburg. When combined with southern Indiana's pre-existing Democratic Party leanings, it is not difficult to imagine political strife leading to trouble in the river towns on the Ohio. Did the two younger men, Hamp Carney and Andrew Mefford, come under the influence of the older Kentucky native and Mexican War veteran? The Carney family, Ohio natives tracing roots to Pennsylvania, would seem unlikely to harbor deep Confederate sympathies. Add the fact that three of Hamp Carney's brothers—William, John R., and George—were Federal soldiers, and it seems reasonable that Elliott Mefford was the prime mover in the Newburg conspiracy, but there is no hard evidence left to support the thought.

Conspiracy Enacted

As reported in the *Daily Evansville Journal*, Johnson's Henderson occupation on July 17 was widely known up and down the river by that same afternoon. If the Meffords and Carney wanted to know where Johnson was, they would have had no problem finding him on the 17th. It just wasn't likely that Indiana residents would have found his roving Kentucky headquarters any earlier in July, although they may have searched for it.

There are two pieces of circumstantial evidence that may refer to the conspirators' hunt for Johnson earlier. On July 4, Governor Morton's secretary forwarded a telegram to Morton in Cleveland, Ohio:

> "It is reported that they [the Rebels] have established friendly communication with sympathizers in Warrick County."

This note appears to refer to open disaffection in Warrick County by Confederate sympathizers. Were the Meffords and Carney vocal enough to be heard all the way to Morton's hotel in Ohio? Were they involved in any "communication" with the Rebels in early July? It's possible, but we don't know.

There is another intriguing reference in the *Daily Evansville Journal* of July 25, 1862:

> "Those two men who were shot in Newburg for piloting Johnson's thieves and robbers across the river spent a day or two in sweet secesh Uniontown [Union County, Kentucky], among some of their friends, to the great annoyance of the good people living there."

Partisan Rangers, page 351, implies that Johnson was in Union County recruiting for a few days after the Henderson attack, perhaps between July 8 and 11. Of course, it could all just be rumor and speculation.

Regardless of these enticing clues of an earlier meeting between the Meffords, Carney, and Johnson, the only date that squares with Johnson's memoir is July 17, 1862. That date provided the notoriety to mark his location to anyone along the lower Ohio River and is the only one that agrees with Johnson's written recollection.

The raid on Newburg was a complex operation with a dozen possible deal-breakers upon thorough analysis. But Adam Johnson never thought like that. For Johnson to put himself in the hands of strangers was nothing unusual; impulsively jumping at an attractive idea was routine for him. Johnson always thought there was more to lose by indecision than by choosing the wrong path. He saw things only as opportunities for positive outcomes. It was a psyche that propelled his success during the war and after it as a blind husband, father, town founder, and businessman. A catalyst can only bring about a reaction when in the presence of the correct element. The Meffords and Carney were that catalyst, and Johnson was the ready, heated element.

The Soldiers at Newburg on July 18, 1862

One of the most common sources of confusion about the Newburg raid emanates from the debate over how many Union soldiers were in the two Newburg hospitals the day of the attack. Several sources put the figure at about 85 soldiers; other sources put the figure variously at 135, 180, 250, and more. Naturally, the greater the number, the greater the disgrace in the surrender.

The most reliable information now available indicates that there were approximately eighty-five soldiers combined at the converted Exchange Hotel and the Frame family house on the day of the raid. Contemporary sources, with one notable exception, all put the figure between eighty and ninety men. The only source that consistently puts the figure higher is Adam Johnson.

The *Daily Evansville Journal*, a source known to have conferred with passengers on the steamer *Eugene* after its trip to Newburg the evening of the raid, puts the first reported figure at 85 on July 19, 1862. The *Henderson Weekly Reporter* repeats the *Daily Evansville Journal* figure and adds in its July 24, 1862, issue that Johnson "claimed to have paroled 135." Johnson's official communication to General Breckinridge of July 21, 1862, puts the figure at 180.

Governor Morton unwittingly supplemented the confusion by reporting to Secretary of War Stanton on July 18 that they had "taken two hundred and fifty of our sick in hospital prisoners. They took 250 arms, destroyed the hospital stores." This communication to Stanton can now be seen in context as a muddled interpretation of a previous telegram received just beforehand by the governor from Legion General Blythe in Evansville giving the first details on the raid. Blythe's telegram to Morton said, "Guerrillas destroyed hospital stores at Newburg, took 250 stands of arms, inmates of hospital taken prisoner, one man killed." Morton mistakenly applied the "250 stands of arms" taken to the number of soldiers in the hospital. In fact, on the nineteenth, after things had settled following the initial confusion, Morton sent another telegram to Secretary Stanton specifically correcting the point by stating, "The Rebels seized Newburg...capturing a hospital with 80 sick and wounded soldiers." After the war, the Indiana Adjutant General's Report on the Newburg raid also puts the quantity of Newburg soldiers at "between eighty or ninety." Kentucky historian E. L. Starling is no help on the subject as he recounts the figure to be both 80 and 180 in his descriptions in *Partisan Rangers*, but he does seem to confirm the figure at 80 in his *History of Henderson County, Kentucky*, which was written much closer to events in 1887. Reid's research in *Newburgh Raid* also puts the figure at 80.

As previously stated, Johnson's estimations are characteristically inflated both in his official communications and throughout *Partisan Rangers*. This is not unexpected. It is a common characteristic of military commanders, then and now, to over-report the numbers of men captured, casualties inflicted, and stores taken. With the pale of forty-two years, it is easy to see how numbers can become hazy. Certainly there was no crucial point at stake for Johnson in getting an exact number for his reports or memoirs. For him, the point was that he captured many men. Indeed, he states in his memoirs that he left the completion of the parole process to Martin on the day of the raid; therefore, in the confusion of events, he may never have had an opportunity to make a complete head count himself. Johnson's natural motivations would lead him to casually boost the number of soldiers captured for both recruitment and publicity purposes.

Finally, Starling and others have surfaced the theory that there were some one hundred active-duty Union soldiers guarding the sick and wounded Newburg convalescents and that Johnson had captured these guards with the hospitalized men, thus explaining the larger number. This idea does not sufficiently account for the activities underway in Indiana in the days just before the raid. Telegrams indicate that every available Indiana soldier had been sent to Kentucky to thwart Morgan's Summer Raid of 1862. Morton's telegram of July 14, quoted in the body of the story, is clear on this point. "The people of the border counties must organize for their own defense. I have no troops that I can send for their defense." The idea that a full company of regular army soldiers would be assigned to such light duty in Newburg (rather than needy Evansville) when Morton was rounding up soldiers from far and wide to send to Kentucky doesn't seem reasonable. Other than Johnson's report to Breckinridge, there is no other meaningful source for a figure higher than eighty-five men.

In the wake of the Newburg raid, all manner of numbers were stated for the soldiers in the town hospitals. Taken as a whole, the figure of approximately eighty-five recovering soldiers seems to be the most likely number in the hospitals on the day of the raid. Even this number was plenty enough for Johnson to claim decisive victory at the Confederate raid on Newburg, Indiana.

A Short Analysis of Sources

In writing this account I have used dozens of sources, but the two most important are Adam Johnson's autobiography, *Partisan Rangers of the Confederate States Army*, and the newspaper accounts of the *Daily Evansville Journal*. These sources are both a blessing and a curse. Without them, we have no story to tell; with them, we know not what we have. Both sources require corroboration, and both have definite points of view.

Adam Johnson wrote his autobiography some forty years after the Newburg events. It is clear now that Johnson had been sharing his wartime recollections with friends and business associates for many years while in Texas after the war. It is very likely that Edmund Starling, author of the 1887 *History of Henderson County, Kentucky*, and Mary Elizabeth Badger, author of an article titled "Thrilling Heroism of Confederates" in the December 1900 issue of the *Confederate Veteran Magazine*, communicated with Johnson about his early Breckinridge Guard days. Johnson in turn seems to have borrowed heavily from both these handy, previously published sources while reconstructing the events of June and July 1862 for his autobiography. In some cases, his account in *Partisan Rangers* incorporates direct quotes from Badger's article.

Johnson's personality as a "big picture" person who cared little for exact dates or details means that *Partisan Rangers* is a work that puts down the story cornerstones and suggests its structure. His estimation of enemy numbers is typically inflated, and on occasion coincidence is touted as intent. His story omissions are as important as his commissions. This is typical of military reports then and since. Johnson does not approach his life as a dispassionate historian, and why should he! With that said, Johnson almost always had his sequence of events in order and did take some pains to get things right when he was making official reports to his superiors during the war. Notwithstanding the information gaps and his strong point of view, Johnson comes through as an entirely compelling character bent on forcing the direction of events taking place during the first two parts of this work. None can doubt, despite any inaccuracy, that Johnson was the single most important figure in Civil War events in northwestern Kentucky between

June 1 and July 19, 1862. Thereafter, Indiana Governor Morton and the soldiers he placed in the Henderson area drove events. Johnson did not disappear—far from it—but his base and focus of operations moved away from Henderson for long periods afterward.

The *Daily Evansville Journal* of 1862 was a single sheet of cotton rag paper, printed on both sides and measuring thirty-two inches long and twenty-one inches tall. The paper was folded longitudinally in the center, thus giving four printed pages of type. As was typical for the day, approximately 50 percent of the newsprint was business advertisements. What was left of the newspaper was a very strong pro-Union—some would say an Abolitionist—newspaper. *Daily Evansville Journal* correspondents interviewed citizens who were on the steamer *Eugene* as it came back from Newburg late on the evening of the raid and were on the *Horner* as it took the Union Rifles of Terre Haute looking for Rebels the next day. These are the most contemporary, available sources to us today. To the *Journal*, Johnson was a "hospital robber"; we would hear no milder characterization of our national enemies today. To the Southern men of Kentucky, he was a military genius. Human history is all points of view. In a final and ironic twist, John Watson Foster would go on to become the editor of the *Daily Evansville Journal* for the four years directly after the war. Under the tutelage of his new mentor—Governor, then U.S. Senator, Morton—Foster's tenure at the prominent southern Indiana newspaper served to launch a political career that would culminate with Foster becoming U.S. secretary of state in the Republican administration of President Benjamin Harrison in 1892.

The *New Albany Daily Ledger* serves as an important source of corroboration for information printed in the *Daily Evansville Journal* during the days following the raid. Although newspapers commonly copy from each other, then and now, this was not always the case for the *Ledger*. The same river pilots who were involved in events at Newburg, Henderson, and Evansville often took news upstream to New Albany, Indiana, and to Louisville, Kentucky, on their mail runs before events were published in the *Journal*. This is confirmed several times, as information regarding events is sometimes published on the same day in both papers with no direct telegraph line between the two cities. In several cases, the *Ledger* directly attributes the information to "a certain steamboatman" coming from the affected locality. Unfortunately, the *Ledger* too is a mixed blessing, confirming events as often as contradicting them.

With regard to the Newburg raid, the *Daily Evansville Journal* was the most well circulated, most reliable, contemporary public information source describing the events of the raid until Terrell's Indiana Adjutant General reports appeared in the late 1860s. Starling's *History of Henderson County, Kentucky* discussed it in some detail twenty-five years after the events, and Johnson's popular autobiography was published in 1904. Then there was a long hiatus in the story with sporadic, short mention in the century since Johnson's memoirs.

I have attempted to add context to the work by beginning with Johnson's activities in the period about three weeks prior to the raid. Careful attention by Newburg authorities to Johnson's attacks at Henderson and Madisonville in the weeks leading up to the Newburg raid could have signaled more vigilance on the part of Home Guard commanders throughout southern Indiana, with possibly a different outcome to the raid. Governor Morton communicated every warning to this effect, and the final fact of a raid on Indiana wasn't likely to have been a surprise to him when it happened. Hindsight has always been our best teacher.

The weeks after the raid are crucial in the instruction they give to us about the fate of western Kentucky in the Civil War. Morton's overwhelmingly forceful reaction to the raid essentially sealed Kentucky west of the Green River for the Union from this point onward in the war. Although things may have been different had the Confederacy won a decisive victory at Perryville, Kentucky, in October 1862, the evacuation of the Confederate army after the battle marked the last serious attempt to bring Kentucky into the Southern fold.

In expanding the scope of the Newburg raid to the shoulder events, several new sources have been introduced to the story—the John Sidney Andrews letters from the Bentley Historical Library, University of Michigan, and the Morton telegrams from the Indiana State Archives can now be examined in context. To me, they enrich the story and amplify events that can now be connected.

Finally, there are *The War of the Rebellion: A Compilation of the Official Records of the Union and Confederate Armies* (which has always been so valuable to the story) and the *Official Records of the Union and Confederate Navies in the War of the Rebellion* (which up to now has been overlooked, but contains several vital communications about events after the raid during the Union reoccupation of Henderson). My thanks to the Cornell University Library program, "Making of America," which put all volumes of these two works in my hands at my home, anytime, via the Internet.

Books like this one sometimes have the effect of bringing forth new sources from the long-forgotten depths of hiding. I hope that proves true in this case. As previously stated, understanding human history is a process, and new information is the fuel that drives the process on. Assembling events helps us assemble the people behind them. Arriving at an understanding of the human condition in any context tells us something about the world in which we live today. In that sense, the dead are a part of our lives and deserve attention on that accord alone, if for no other.

Echoes of '62

Even now, with the sesquicentennial of the raid approaching, it is possible to hear the echo of events as they occurred that hot summer day in July. Today, the old town center of Newburgh, Indiana, compromises with its twin identity as an historic slice of Indiana's past within a twenty-first-century neighborhood of automobiles, restaurants, and the accoutrements of modern life. As the siege of residential and commercial development tightens around the old city, the layout of events can still be traced.

The Exchange Hotel, the site of the pivotal showdown between Johnson and the Union soldiers, still stands, albeit somewhat changed from its physical appearance of 140 years ago. Street names are as they were then, and the home of Union Bethell, feared to become cannon fodder on the day of the raid, stands today maintaining its general appearance from the time of the raid. The Old Stone House is now on the National Register of Historic Places. Although the Bethell warehouse that contained Johnson's prized armory is long gone, its approximate location on the waterfront is known. The Rutledge House, known then as the Frame House, the intended destination of the frazzled Dr. Tilman before meeting up with a Confederate picket, is also a beautiful, restored private residence. One can easily get a feel for the distances and can plant one's feet on the spot where Union Bethell must have seen Johnson's log and stovepipe cannons for the first time. You can also get an appreciation for the ride of Dr. Lewis toward downtown Evansville, as Indiana State Road 662 traces the route today.

Recreating the events of Johnson's Henderson attack on the National Hotel in late June 1862 is no problem. Indeed, a building stands today on the spot of the National that could have very easily come straight from the era (but is actually more recent). The location of Alves's Grove and the old Henderson Cemetery are known, and the path taken during the attack by the "band of three" can be confidently surmised. The courthouses in both Evansville and Henderson are post-war replacements, but the current Henderson courthouse is on the same spot where Johnson accepted visitors as Henderson's chief administrator on that humid July day more than a century ago.

Surprisingly, in the face of its contribution in soldiers and sailors, Evansville has a relatively modest output of official Civil War remembrance. But it does have one low, curious block on display near the assembly grounds for the old Evansville Home Guard units. Sitting near the Evansville Museum of Arts and Science is a heavy, shaded, gray monument crowned with a black, rusting 4-pounder cannon barrel. It is dedicated to the memory of the man who, above all contemporaries, embodied Evansville's steamboat heritage—Captain Henry T. Dexter. The memorial succinctly condenses to these words: "Henry T. Dexter—One of the Bravest and most Distinguished Officers on our Western Waters." Dexter's bearded image is barely discernable due to the erosion of time. The memorial rests just one hundred yards or so from the spot where Dexter first learned of the Newburg events. The old Oak Hill Cemetery in Evansville contains, within easy sight of each other, the large tombstones of both Henry Dexter and John Watson Foster. The grave of Frank Owen, Johnson's loyal first recruit, is also in Oak Hill.

The American Midwest is surrounded by a precious gift gone from many of the urban areas of our land—it is surrounded by tangible evidence of its past. Although there are some who would say that the old stones of memory have no ready place in our modern world, I disagree. I say these buildings, these monuments, these memories are the very things upon which our modern-day minds rest and, as such, should be preserved—if not for us, then for our grateful future.

Abbreviations

BHL   Bentley Historical Library, University of Michigan

CR   *The Cannelton Reporter*

DEJ   *The Daily Evansville Journal*

HWR   *The Henderson Weekly Reporter*

IWOR   W. H. H. Terrell, *Indiana in the War of the Rebellion, Report of the Adjutant General of the State of Indiana*, 1869

MTB GD 4   Governor Oliver P. Morton Telegram Book, General Dispatches No. 4, 6–11–62 to 7–31–62. Indiana State Archives, Commission on Public Records

NADL   *The New Albany Daily Ledger*

ORA   *The War of the Rebellion: A Compilation of the Official Records of the Union and Confederate Armies*, 1880–1901

ORN   *Official Records of the Union and Confederate Navies in the War of the Rebellion*, 1894–1922

PR   Adam Rankin Johnson, *Partisan Rangers of the Confederate States Army*, 1904

Reference Notes

♦

BOOK I

Henderson, Kentucky

♦

1. *Daily Evansville Journal* (hereafter referred to as *DEJ*), June 23, 1862; *Henderson Weekly Reporter* (hereafter referred to as *HWR*), June 26, 1862; Letter, G. B. Tyler to J. S. Andrews, date unknown (between June 22 and 29, 1862), John Sidney Andrews Papers, Bentley Historical Library, University of Michigan (hereafter referred to as BHL).

2. *DEJ*, June 23, 1862; *HWR*, June 26, 1862; Richard A. Briggs, *The Saga of Fort Duffield* (West Point, Kentucky, 1999), 76; "Don Harvey, Battery F regimental history," http://www.michiganinthewar.org/artillery/battf.htm (accessed 2003).

3. George Smith diary 1859–1873, May 22, June 12, 1862; *HWR*, June 19, 1862.

4. Maralea Arnett, *The Annals & Scandals of Henderson County, Kentucky 1775–1975* (Corydon, Kentucky, 1976), 41; Mendy Dorris, *Tug of War* (1996), 1; Edmund L. Starling, *History of Henderson County, Kentucky* (Henderson, Kentucky, 1887), 193, 195, 197; Lowell Harrison, *The Civil War in Kentucky* (Louisville, 1975), 1; William A. Degregorio, *The Complete Book of U.S. Presidents* (3rd ed.) (New York, 1992), 234.

5. J. M. Armstrong, *Biographical Encyclopaedia of Kentucky* (1878), 418. The College of New Jersey was later renamed Princeton University; John E. Kleber, *The Kentucky Encyclopedia* (Lexington, Kentucky, 1992), 109.

6. *DEJ*, June 23, 24, 28, 1862; Letter, G. B. Tyler to J. S. Andrews, date unknown, BHL; Adam R. Johnson, *Partisan Rangers of the Confederate States Army* (hereafter referred to as *PR*, originally Louisville, 1904; Austin, Texas, 1995 reprint is used throughout), 92–94.

7. Letter, L. Hale to J. S. Andrews, July 10, 1862, BHL.

8. Letter, G. B. Tyler to J. S. Andrews, date unknown, BHL.

9. *DEJ*, June 26, 1862.

10. Ibid.

11. *DEJ*, June 23, 1862, says Andrews's Battery arrived with fifty men. On June 26 the *DEJ* mentions the Provost Guard arriving with sixty more soldiers. Johnson's intelligence from *PR* (95) put the total at eighty.

12. George Smith diary, June 28, 30, July 4, 1862; *DEJ*, June 27, 1862; Letter, L. Hale to J. S. Andrews, July 8, 1862, BHL.

13. *PR*, 475.

14. *PR*, 1, 253; E. Polk Johnson, *History of Kentucky and Kentuckians*, vol. 2 (Chicago, New York, 1912), 1003.

15. *PR*, 253.

16. Starling, 804–805; *PR*, 2, 82–85. Johnson met Breckinridge for the first time on the day after the Battle of Farmington, Mississippi—May 10, 1862.

17. *PR*, 38; Photograph of William S. Johnson is between *PR* pages 48 and 49; Starling, 714.

18. *PR*, 90.

19. *PR*, 40.

20. *PR*, 91, 285, 395–405. Francis Amplias "Frank" Owen was part of the 8th Confederate Kentucky Infantry Regiment, Company A. Several other soldiers from the 8th Confederate Kentucky would eventually join the Partisan Rangers. Owen's account in Part II of *Partisan Rangers* was meant to fill in event dates where Johnson's narrative was lacking. Unfortunately, Owen's event dates are sorely inaccurate.

21. *PR*, 92–94, 245; *DEJ*, June 28, 1862; Mary Elizabeth Badger, "Thrilling Heroism of Confederates," *Confederate Veteran Magazine*, vol. 8, December 1900 (Broadfoot Bookmark, Wendell, North Carolina), 525.

22. *PR*, 95; *DEJ*, July 2, 1862. Colonel Shackelford flatly stated at the Henderson meeting the day after the attack, "a part of these outlaws, who committed a diabolical murder in the very heart of the city, had been entertained by citizens of Henderson on Sunday."

23. *DEJ*, June 30, 1862.

24. *PR*, 95; Mendy Dorris and Linda Hallmark, *Henderson County, Kentucky, Civil War Walking and/or Driving Tour* (pamphlet, 1998).

25. *PR*, 95–96; Letter, L. Hale to J. S. Andrews, July 8, 1862, BHL; Badger, 525; *Confederate Veteran Magazine*, vol. 6, March 1898, 114.

26. *PR*, 96; *DEJ*, July 1, 1862; *HWR*, July 3, 1862; Badger, 525; Letter, L. Hale to J. S. Andrews, July 8, 1862, BHL.

27. Badger, 525; *DEJ*, July 1, 1862, is at odds with Johnson's account from *Partisan Rangers*. The *DEJ* states that Captain Daly anticipated the attack, and Hale's July 8 letter to Captain Andrews states that the men were instructed to sleep on their arms. However, despite some apparent forewarning, the two Dalys and a number of others were seated outside the hotel, without pickets, enveloped by darkness on all sides except for a single streetlight.

28. Letter, L. Hale to J. S. Andrews, July 8, 1862, BHL. Johnson refers to his victim as Lieutenant Lyon in *PR*, 96—it was actually Lieutenant Tyler. This inaccuracy was first published in "Thrilling Heroism of Confederates," *Confederate Veteran Magazine*, vol. 8, December 1900, 525–527. The article is attributed to Mary Elizabeth Badger, but the ultimate source of the information may be Adam Johnson. *PR* (225) states that several

members of the Badger family were business associates of Johnson's after the war. The *Confederate Veteran* article contains much that later went into *Partisan Rangers*.

29. Badger, 525; *PR*, 96; John Taylor Hatchett, "What I Remember About The Civil War," January 1929, as printed in Mendy Dorris's *Tug of War*, 73.

30. *New Albany Daily Ledger* (hereafter referred to as *NADL*), July 2, 1862. For more on the *John T. McCombs* see *Frederick Way's Packet Directory 1848–1994*, boat #3120. This paragraph is assembled from references noting that the *McCombs* routinely berthed at either Henderson or Louisville, that Captain Ballard was the pilot of the *McCombs*, and that the *McCombs* delivered the wounded soldiers to Louisville from Henderson. The captain certainly would have heard the racket caused by the attack and rumors were circulating by daybreak on June 30.

31. *PR*, 96; *HWR*, July 3, 1862; *NADL*, July 2, 1862.

32. Lewis Kiner's unit is a guess because, under this spelling, he is not listed on the roster of either the Provost Guard or Battery F. "Lewis L. Kline" is listed with the 1st Michigan Light Artillery, and I'm guessing this is he; *HWR*, July 3, 1862. Some of the soldiers' first names may be incorrect in the *HWR* report; Letter, L. Hale to J. S. Andrews, July 10, 1862, BHL; *DEJ*, July 1, 1862; *NADL*, July 2, 1862. Griffin was later released and became a member of the Partisan Rangers, Company B.

33. *DEJ*, July 1, 1862, lists the casualty count as eleven wounded and one dead. The *HWR*, July 3, 1862, has a more balanced account and has the advantage of being on the scene. Johnson to Breckinridge, July 21, 1862, *The War of the Rebellion: A Compilation of the Official Records of the Union and Confederate Armies* (hereafter referred to as *ORA*), vol. 16, chap. 28, pt. 2, 994.

34. *HWR*, July 3, 1862; *DEJ*, July 2, 1862.

35. *PR*, 102, 258–259, 310; Starling, 202; *DEJ*, July 2, August 21, 1862; *HWR*, July 3, 1862.

36. *HWR*, July 3, 1862.

37. Colonel James Murrell Shackelford was a lawyer and Mexican War veteran who was colonel of the 25th Union Kentucky Infantry. He resigned in March 1862. In August 1862, he volunteered to raise the 8th Union Kentucky Cavalry, partly in response to the success of Adam Johnson in western Kentucky. He later became brigadier general.

38. *HWR*, July 3, 1862.

39. *DEJ*, July 2, 1862; Archibald Dixon was elected Kentucky lieutenant governor, 1844–1848, and was appointed U.S. senator from Kentucky, 1852–1855.

40. *HWR*, July 3, 1862; *NADL*, July 2, 1862.

41. *HWR*, July 3, 1862; *DEJ*, July 1, 1862. Johnson's remembrance of the *DEJ* article as published in *PR* (97) is inaccurate. The estimated enemy strength stated in the *DEJ* article was not 300, but rather 150, still impressive. This is another error traceable to *Confederate Veteran*, vol. 8, December 1900, 525–527.

42. *DEJ*, July 2, 11, 1862.

43. *DEJ*, July 2, 1862; *NADL*, July 3, 1862.

44. *DEJ*, July 3, 1862; *NADL*, July 3, 1862.

45. Blythe to Morton, July 1, 1862, Governor Oliver P. Morton Telegram Book, General Dispatches No. 4 (hereafter referred to as MTB GD 4); *Indiana Magazine of History*, vol. 40, June 1944, 61, for reference to Blythe's election to the Indiana State House of Representatives for the 1847–1848 term. Blythe commanded all Indiana Legion (Home Guard) regiments in Posey, Vanderburgh, Gibson, Warrick, Spencer, Pike, Dubois, and Knox Counties.

46. Terrell to Morton, July 2, 1862, MTB GD 4; Blythe to Love, July 3, 1862, MTB GD 4.

47. *DEJ*, July 5, 1862; Daniel W. Snepp, *Sidelights of Early Evansville History* (1974), 18. "A packet boat is one that travels a regular schedule between ports carrying passengers, freight, and mail."

48. Biographical sketch from Edward White, "Captain Henry T. Dexter," *Evansville and Its Men of Mark* (Evansville, 1873), 62–65; F. M. Gilbert, "Who Captain Dexter Was," *Evansville Courier*, July 31, 1910; "Browning People Study" notecard in the Evansville–Vanderburgh Central Library, Evansville, Indiana; Details on the *Courier* from Way, boat #1353; Augustus J. Lemcke, *Reminiscences of an Indianian* (Indianapolis, 1905), 38, 190. Later in the war, Dexter was scammed with a bogus tip on a trotter named "John A. Logan." He lost his life savings, $50,000; *Indiana Magazine of History*, "Evansville Steamboats During the Civil War," December 1941, 366; *DEJ*, July 5, 1862.

49. *DEJ*, July 5, 1862.

50. *PR*, 90, 100–101. Johnson says he had "six men to depend on" in *PR*, 101. His official 1862 report says there were five and he.

51. Blythe to Indianapolis, July 4, 1862, MTB GD 4.

52. Love to Blythe, July 4, 5, 1862, MTB GD 4; Blythe to Love, July 4, 1862, MTB GD 4. Mount Vernon, Indiana, is a small Ohio River community approximately twenty miles west of Evansville.

53. Edison H. Thomas, *John Hunt Morgan and His Raiders* (Lexington, 1975), 39; *PR*, 359.

54. Thomas Lawrence Connelly, *Army of the Heartland, The Army of Tennessee, 1861–1862* (Baton Rouge and London, 1967), 200–201.

55. *PR*, 402; Johnson to Breckinridge, July 21, 1862, *ORA*, vol. 16 chap. 28, pt. 2, 994. Johnson identifies July 5 as the day of the Madisonville mission. *PR*, 128 indicates the attack was at midnight. This is substantially corroborated by a Union soldier's diary entry in John W. Rowell, *Yankee Cavalryman; Through the Civil War with the Ninth Pennsylvania Cavalry* (Knoxville, 1971), 55; Frank Owen's Oak Hill Cemetery, Evansville, Indiana, internment record, 1909.

56. *DEJ*, July 31, 1862. The location of the Union camp in Madisonville is well-known, and the geography is described through a personal visit to the site.

57. *PR*, 101–102; Badger, 526; Johnson to Breckinridge, July 21, 1862, *ORA*, vol. 16, chap. 28, pt. 2, 994. Johnson names A. W. Ray, John Donaly (Donley), Marion Myers, William Halis (Hollis), Bob Martin, and himself as the Madisonville combatants, a total of six. Forty-two years later in *Partisan Rangers*, he names Bob Martin, Jake Bennett, Frank Owen, Tom Gooch, John Connelly (probably meant Donley), Marion Myers, and himself, a total of seven—another likely *Partisan Ranger* inaccuracy traceable to Mary Elizabeth Badger.

58. *PR*, 100–101.

59. Badger, 526; *PR*, 101–102; Rowell, 55.

60. Rowell, 55.

61. Badger, 526; *PR*, 102; Rowell, 60. Johnson implies that the Union commander was stationed in the town of Madisonville rather than at the Browning Farm with his men at the time of the attack. This is corroborated in Rowell. The Eagle Hotel would have been the only logical location in town.

62. This scene is assembled, as there is no documentation for Union Bethell's inner thoughts. As a wealthy businessman and Home Guard captain, he no doubt subscribed to the *Daily Evansville Journal* and certainly knew of Johnson's June Henderson attack from the heavy reporting it received. That attack no doubt got his attention, but the total lack of preparation on July 18 infers that nothing much was done despite the news.

   Evansville Press, June 9, 1972. The "Old Sandstone Mansion" is the home now known as the "Old Stone House." Union Noble Bethell, the son of Union Bethell, confirmed that he was born in the "Old Stone House" in 1859 and lived there for fourteen years until his parents moved closer to town to what is now known as the "Union Bethell House" on Main Street, Newburgh. The Old Stone House, which was built with large quantities of Cannelton, Indiana, sandstone in the 1830s, was listed on the National Register of Historic Places in 1975. Steamboat cargo manifests indicate that the annual wheat harvest came in at this time of year.

63. *PR*, 97–98, 247; Starling 655, 766–767. Johnson's mother, Juliet Spencer Rankin, and Barrett's wife, Susan Daniel Rankin, were half sisters. George Hatchett, Phillip Matthews, and John Barrett were Virginia natives. Henderson County Genealogical Society, *175th Anniversary of Kentucky Historical and Biographical Notes* (Henderson, 1967).

64. *PR*, 97–98, 247; *HWR*, July 3, 1862.

65. Johnson says he wrote the letter on July 10, 1862, in *Partisan Rangers*, page 97, and then paraphrases the contents. The entire note is printed in full and dated July 6, 1862, in *PR*, 247–248. It appeared in *HWR*, July 10, 1862, and in *DEJ*, July 16, 1862.

66. *PR*, 247–248; *DEJ*, July 16, 1862.

67. *PR*, 49, 250–251, 254–255. Dixon's reply to Johnson contains the phrase, "since I knew you." Starling acknowledges Dixon's "touching" reference, "to the days he knew Colonel Johnson and his high honor."

68. *PR*, 248–249. All quoted replies to Johnson in *HWR*, July 17, 1862.

69. *HWR*, July 10, 1862; Letter, L. Hale to J. S. Andrews, July 10, 1862, BHL.

70. *HWR*, July 10, 1862; *NADL*, July 7, 1862.

71. *A Biographical History of Eminent and Self-Made Men of the State of Indiana*, vol. 1, seventh district, 128–131.

72. *DEJ*, July 8, 11, 1862; *HWR*, July 10, 1862; *NADL*, July 7, 1862; Love to Morton, July 8, 11, 1862, MTB GD 4; Morton to Love, July 11, 1862, MTB GD 4.

73. *DEJ*, July 14, 1862; *NADL*, July 12, 1862; Rowell, 62–67; Gano to Morgan, July 1862, *ORA*, vol. 16, chap. 28, pt. 1, 771–774; Morgan to Smith, July 9, 1862, *ORA*, vol. 16, chap. 28, pt. 1, 766–767. This was revenge for Morgan. Jordan's men were part of the cavalry brigade that ambushed Morgan's Raiders on May 4 and 5 at Lebanon, Tennessee, at what came to be known as the "Lebanon Races"; Thomas, 41. "Bull Pups" were the nicknames for Morgan's two light artillery pieces.

74. Boyle to Buell, July 10, 1862, *ORA*, vol. 16, chap. 28, pt. 1, 731–732; Boyle to Stanton, July 10, 1862, *ORA*, vol. 16, chap. 28, pt. 1, 732; Boyle to Halleck, July 12, 1862, *ORA*, vol. 16, chap. 28, pt. 1, 734; Boyle to Hatch, July 12, 1862, *ORA*, vol. 16, chap. 28, pt. 1, 735; Boyle to Lincoln, July 13, 1862, *ORA*, vol. 16, chap. 28, pt. 1, 737; Lincoln to Boyle, July 13, 1862, *ORA*, vol. 16, chap. 28, pt. 1, 738. Lincoln, with typical aplomb, replies to Boyle by telling him to "call on General Halleck ... I have telegraphed him you are in trouble."

75. Letters, L. Hale to J. S. Andrews, July 10, 11, 1862, BHL.

76. Letters, L. Hale to J. S. Andrews, July 8, 10, 11, 1862, BHL; See the Branch County, Michigan, Marriage Index for the marriage records of Luther F. Hale and Louisa G. Fischer, married February 10, 1850. Within a few weeks Battery F would obtain its artillery weapons only to have them captured during the Battle of Richmond, Kentucky, at the end of August 1862. Hale would become battery captain in October upon Andrews's resignation. Hale was promoted again, to major, in December 1862 and finished the war at the rank of lieutenant colonel.

77. Letter, L. Hale to J. S. Andrews, July 11, 1862, BHL; *DEJ*, July 11, 14, 1862. Nicklin was carrying several shotguns and a set of breastplates captured from a man arrested on one of Nicklin's raids; General Love was also present at the same gathering to give one of his speeches in conjunction with his inspection tour of the Home Guard units previously mentioned; Boyle to Stanton, July 13, 1862, *ORA*, vol. 16, chap. 28, pt. 1, 738. Boyle makes reference to the "small force at...Henderson"; Boyle to Stanton, July 14, 1862, *ORA*, vol. 16, chap. 28, pt. 1, 739–740. Boyle says he has withdrawn the force at Henderson; G. C. Smith to Boyle, July 26, 1862, *ORA*, vol. 16, chap. 28, pt. 1, 759–762.

78. Morris S. Johnson to Morton, July 12, 1862, MTB GD 4.

79. *DEJ*, July 15, 16, 1862; George Smith diary, July 15, 1862; Rowell, 69; *NADL*, July 15, 17, 1862; Boyle to Greene, July 12, 1862, *ORA*, vol. 16, chap. 28, pt. 1, 734; G. C. Smith to Boyle, July 26, 1862, *ORA*, vol. 16, chap. 28, pt. 1, 759–762. General Smith implies he left Henderson on July 13, but the *DEJ* indicates he left July 14.

80. Rowell, 69.

81. Derived from Johnson's statements in *PR*, 102, and Rowell, 68–69. Johnson states that he put a tail on Union troops within an hour of the Federals leaving Madisonville (he probably did so as they passed Slaughtersville). Johnson identifies the 9th Pennsylvania Cavalry as the unit he attacked at Browning Springs in the photo between *PR* pages 120 and 121, and on 128; *PR*, 301. The "Dutch Cavalry" was the nickname Johnson's men gave to the 9th Pennsylvania Cavalry Regiment.

82. Morton to Blythe, July 14, 1862, MTB GD 4.

83. *DEJ*, July 17, 1862, wryly notes that, "It would have been far better never to have sent any troops into that region than to withdraw them after they had begun their work of making arrests"; Boyle to Stanton, July 17, 1862, *ORA*, vol. 16, chap. 28, pt. 1, 744. "They [the Rebels] have driven off the best Union men at Henderson, on the Ohio River."

84. *PR*, 102; *DEJ*, July 18, 1862.

85. *HWR*, July 24, 1862; *DEJ*, July 19, 21, 1862; *NADL*, July 19, 1862.

86. *PR*, 102–103, 258–259, 275–277; Starling, 751–752; *NADL*, July 21, 1862.

87. *DEJ*, July 18, 1862; *PR*, 251–252.

88. *DEJ*, July 18, 19, 1862.

89. *NADL*, July 19, 1862; Starling, 749–750; *PR*, 102–104, 128. Also, *Dictionary of American Naval Fighting Ships*, vol. 1B, 157, for information on the *U.S. Brilliant*; *PR*, 103 and 345 indicate that the "flag was raised over the courthouse," but it is unclear whether this was a physical or a metaphorical description. *HWR*, July 24, 1862, reports the flag was planted in the ground at the courthouse gate. It's possible the flag, which was probably not a full-sized battle flag, was moved around for a time, possibly also to the Hancock House. It is possible that the flag merely "reigned" over the courthouse for the day.

♦

BOOK II
Newburg, Indiana

♦

1. Arnett, 254; Starling, 396–401. The Scuffletown, Kentucky, population was proba-
    bly less than one hundred at this time. The great Ohio River flood of 1937 perma-
    nently wiped out the town.

    John Darby's occupation, genealogy, military career, and whereabouts are woven
    together for this account. No documentation exists for his inner thoughts. This scene
    is assembled from photographs of the era, the fact that Darby arrived home from
    Shiloh on a steamer after his resignation (probably around May 1, 1862), and the pre-
    sumption that he was happy to be home.

2. The *Newburgh Register* of November 30, 1967, discusses the discovery in Warrick
    County of a special 1859 census of all persons inside the consolidated city of
    Newburg conducted by Edwin Adams on February 15, 1859. At that time, the pop-
    ulation was 797; Darrel E. Bigham, *Towns and Villages of the Lower Ohio* puts the 1860
    Newburg population at 999; Goodspeed Brothers, *History of Warrick, Spencer, and
    Perry Counties* (Chicago, 1885), 21; Crenshaw, Parker, Forsythe, and Tromly, *Historical
    Markers Erected by the Women's Club of Newburgh, Indiana, 1975–1979* (date not given),
    22; Edwin Adams, *History of Warrick County, Indiana* (1868), 41. Sprinkle arrived in
    1803 and laid out the town in 1817. The "h" at the end of Newburgh was added in
    1928 to clear up postal mishaps with Newberry, Indiana.

3. Crenshaw, et al., 22; Darby's occupation is listed as cabinetmaker in Oscar J. Phillips
    and Opal B. Phillips's *Warrick County, Indiana, 1850 Census* (Owensboro, Kentucky,
    1980); He is listed as a carpenter in the *Warrick County, Indiana, 1860 Federal Census*,
    Captain Jacob Warrick Chapter of the National Association of the Daughters of the
    American Revolution, Boonville, Indiana (Owensboro, Kentucky, 1981). Darby's War
    Department archive notes unspecified "family affairs" as his reason for resignation.

4. Adams, 77; Adah Jackson, "Glimpses of Civil War Newburg, An Account of Eliza
    Bethell Warren's Girlhood in Newburgh, Indiana, 1855–1870," *Indiana Magazine of
    History*, vol. 41, no. 2, June, 1945, 169; Daniel W. Snepp, "Evansville's Channels of
    Trade and the Secessionist Movement, 1850–1865," Indiana Historical Society
    Publications, vol. 8, no. 7, (Indianapolis, 1928), 373.

5. *Inventory of the County Archives of Indiana, No. 87, Warrick County, Boonville*
    (Indianapolis, 1940), 15; Snepp, *Sidelights of Early Evansville History*, 30.

6. W. H. H. Terrell, *Report of the Adjutant General of the State of Indiana*, vol. 3
    (Indianapolis, 1866), 543–544; W. H. H. Terrell, *Indiana in the War of the Rebellion*
    (hereafter referred to as *IWOR*, Indianapolis, 1869), vol. 1, 148–150. The Newburg

Home Guards organized July 8, 1861; the Boonville Home Guards, Warrick Home Guards, Newburg Grays, and Warrick Rangers organized October 10, 1861; the Yankeetown Home Guards organized October 12, 1861, and the Campbell Township Guards organized on October 22, 1861; Jackson, 177.

7. A pension affidavit in John Darby's War Department archive indicates that the soldiers blamed their illness on rebels poisoning a stream from which they had taken water. It's more likely they contracted diarrhea from local bacteria and impurities; Veatch to Lauman, February 18, 1862, *ORA*, vol. 7, chap. 17, 227–229; Adams's *History of Warrick County, Indiana*, 73, says Darby resigned from Company H in August 1861—his official War Department archive clearly shows him resigning on April 20, 1862.

8. Darby's presence on the Shiloh battlefield is derived from his War Department archive. The 25th Indiana arrived at Pittsburg Landing (Shiloh), Tennessee, on March 18, 1862. Darby was "present" for roll call on March 31, 1862, and resigned April 20, 1862. Other than army diarrhea, he had no other recorded illness in the interim; *DEJ*, April 14, 1862, John Watson Foster's published letter to his father regarding the Shiloh battle; Veatch to Atkins, April 10, 1862, *ORA*, vol. 10, chap. 22, pt. 1, 222–223. The regiment entered the field that day with 651 soldiers. Of those, 23 were killed, 103 were wounded, and 13 were missing in action; Foster to Veatch, April 11, 1862, *ORA*, vol. 10, chap. 22, pt. 1, 230–232. Darby "seeing" Lt. Dorus Fellows's wound is derived from company command structure and the solid presumption, previously discussed, that Darby was on the battlefield; Fellows's wound is characterized as "mortal" by McReynolds in his "A Boy's Recollections of the Civil War," *Colorado Springs Evening Sun*, 1905; *The Newburgh, Indiana, Sesquicentennial, 1803–1953*, 37, notes that Fellows died on June 21, 1862, of his Shiloh wounds; Wiley Sword, *Shiloh: Bloody April* (Morningside House, Dayton, Ohio, 2001), 263–266.

9. Daniel W. Snepp, *John W. Foster, Evansville's Distinguished Citizen* (1975), 9–10.

10. *DEJ*, April 14, 1862, John Watson Foster's long letter to his father; Snepp, *John W. Foster, Evansville's Distinguished Citizen*, 14–15; Veatch to Atkins, April 10, 1862, *ORA*, vol. 10, chap. 22, pt. 1, 222. Foster would be promoted to lieutenant colonel April 30, 1862, for his brave performance at Shiloh.

11. Terrell, *IWOR*, vol. 1, 148–150.

12. Family histories written by Union Noble Bethell dated April 30, 1927, and June 1, 1932. Union Noble Bethell (1859–1933) was the son of Union Bethell (1826–1907). The Bethell family lineage is one of the oldest in European America. As might be expected, with nearly 400 years of sometimes scantily documented history, there are some inconsistencies in the information. Most of the information for this book comes from a family-tree synopsis put together by the esteemed Union Noble Bethell. Union Noble Bethell compiled his last, and perhaps most complete, account of his family background just months before his death. In retirement, genealogy had become a pas-

sion for Union Noble, and he had the resources to search things out. Union Noble specifically states that Sampson's participation in the Revolutionary War was strictly family lore with no official record. Since 1932, much new information about the Bethells has been uncovered. Some doubt has been raised about Sampson's participation in the Revolutionary War.

13. Jackson, 169–170; Goodspeed Brothers, 93; *Evansville Courier & Journal*, November 2, 1924; Letters of John W. Keller, 16th U.S. Infantry Regiment.

14. Biographical sketch of Thomas Bethell from a family history written by Union Noble Bethell, dated June 1, 1932; Jackson, 170–177; *Warrick County, Indiana, 1860 Federal Census.*

15. Phillips and Phillips's, *Warrick County, Indiana, 1850 Census* has a blank space next to Union Bethell's occupation; Barbara Smith, *Warrick County, Indiana, 1850 Census* lists Union Bethell's occupation as "none"; *Boonville Enquirer*, April 4, 1896. Union Bethell is identified as being someone with a long Republican history who was elected to the office of Warrick County Auditor on the Republican ticket in years past. He also was accused of doing a great deal of "scolding and punching of certain Democrats in Warrick and Spencer Counties."

16. Jackson, 176–177; William Burleigh, *A Bicentennial Look at Newburgh, Indiana, 1776–1976* (Newburgh, Indiana, 1976), 44; Bethell–Warren Papers, Union Bethell Day Book, 1860–1880, William Henry Smith Memorial Library, Indiana Historical Society Archives.

17. *Warrick County, Indiana, 1860 Federal Census.*

18. *DEJ*, June 7, 1862.

19. Ibid.

20. Starling, 770; *Memoirs of the Lower Ohio Valley* (Madison, Wisconsin, 1905), 36; For a folk-art sketch of the Soaper Farm circa 1880 see D. J. Lake & Co., *An Illustrated Historical Atlas of Henderson and Union Counties, Kentucky* (Philadelphia, 1880).

21. *PR*, 237; Starling, 626.

22. *PR*, 104. "While at the Soaper farm…I was informed that there were hundreds of stands of guns in the arsenal of this town (Newburg)…" This is as close as Johnson ever gets to acknowledging the help of Mefford and Carney. Starling refers to them as "two men who had been pressed into service by Johnson" in *PR*, 235; Carney and Mefford were first named as the two "who came over the river with the guerrillas" in the *DEJ* of July 19, 1862.

23. Goodspeed Brothers, 93; No documentation exists for the details of these conversations, but given the outcome the next day there is little doubt about the content of the discussions.

24. *PR*, 254.

25. D. J. Lake & Co., *An Illustrated Historical Atlas of Henderson County, Kentucky*, (Philadelphia, 1880) shows the crossroad leading up to the mouth of the Green River; *PR*, 104. "As soon as the men had eaten supper, I gave the command to saddle up...." They arrived at the Soaper farm in the late afternoon of July 17, probably made fires for food, fed their horses, ate, and relaxed. At this time they were in no hurry. Arriving near Newburg at "ten o'clock next morning," it is presumed that they left in the early morning of July 18.

26. Starling, 396–398.

27. *PR*, 105; The dredged, dammed, and cleared Ohio River of today is quite different than it was more than 140 years ago. It was not unusual in summer for the river level in places between Evansville and Cairo, Illinois, to be a mere two to three feet. *DEJ* reports for the entire week indicate the river level was extremely low; *DEJ*, July 18, 1862. Ironically, the source of the telegraph problem was discovered sometime on the 18th, after the raid. This allowed Governor Morton to receive Evansville telegrams about the attack on that same afternoon.

28. *PR*, 105.

29. Starling, 401; *PR*, 104–105. Martin landed his squad "several squares above," somewhere slightly east of town. The flammable liquid (perhaps turpentine or alcohol spirits?) is confirmed by mention in McReynolds's "A Boy's Recollections of the Civil War." Was this just another ruse? It's possible, but Johnson does not position it as such, whereas the cannons clearly are discussed as a ruse. As a person who kept his eye on the newspapers, Adam Johnson possibly first learned of the "Quaker Cannon" trick when it was used successfully by CSA General Joseph E. Johnston to fool Union General George B. McClellan in the early months of 1862 in Virginia. It's also possible that Johnson came up with it independently, as it was certainly within his normal means.

30. Starling, 715; James L. Head, *The Atonement of John Brooks* (Geneva, Florida, 2001), 45; *PR*, 104–105; Terrell, *IWOR*, vol. 1, 182; Fred Joyce, "Why Sue Mundy Became a Guerrilla" *Southern Bivouac*, vol. 2, no. 3, November 1883, 127; *NADL*, July 21, 1862; State Street ran all the way to the river's edge in those days.

31. *NADL*, July 21, 1862; *PR*, 234, "[T]he Confederates crossed the Ohio River in mid-day by the use of skiffs, scows and old boats"; Darby's resignation was effective April 20, 1862; The *DEJ* of July 25, 1862, refers to former Captain Darby as Captain "Dorley." There is no "Captain Dorley" in the entire Union army according to the National Park Service's Civil War Soldiers and Sailors System. This was no doubt a poor transcription of the cursive "Darby" and explains a long-standing mystery as to why the captain at Newburg refused to take command of Union troops. He was a retired captain. Darby's presence in Warrick County (Newburg) is specifically confirmed by a *DEJ* report of July 15, 1862, where he is nominated for Warrick County coroner. Sergeant Henry may be Newburg resident Sergeant Charles E. Henry, Company I, 25th Indiana Infantry.

32. *DEJ*, July 25, 1862; Burleigh, 193; The National Park Service's Civil War Soldiers and Sailors System lists John R. Tilman as "John P. Tillman." The true spelling from documents signed by Tilman himself and residing with Kay Lant is "Tilman"; William D. Foulke, *The Life of Oliver P. Morton*, Vol. 1, (Indianapolis, 1899), 167–168; Will Fortune, *Warrick and Its Prominent People* (Evansville, Indiana, 1881), 167; Frank Owen and several other future members of the Breckinridge Guards were at Camp Morton at the same time as Dr. Tilman. Had Tilman remained in Newburg that day he may have recognized them.

33. Ironically, Darby would later become captain of the Newburg Blues, a Newburg Home Guard company formed in September 1862. Terrell, *Report of the Adjutant General of the State of Indiana*, vol. 3, 544; *DEJ*, July 25, 1862, Tilman letter to the editor.

34. In *PR* (105 and 128) Johnson puts the total number of men invading Newburg at twenty-seven. This is presumed to be a count that does not include Carney and the Meffords; Charles Emery Johnson, *One Hundred Years of Evansville, Indiana, 1812–1912 with Miscellanea* (1948), 148.

35. Starling, 716; *DEJ*, July 25, 1862; *HWR*, July 24, 1862; In *PR* (106), Johnson states that he faced eighty men at the Exchange Hotel hospital. Evidence shows that there were approximately eighty-five convalescent soldiers at Newburg, but about thirty of these were at the Frame House. This means Johnson would have faced about fifty-five soldiers at the Exchange.

36. *PR*, 106; Starling, 716; The dining room is referred to as the "Long Hall" in *DEJ*, July 25, 1862; A letter to the editor printed in the *DEJ* of July 25, 1862, by S. B. Johnson, the only name that we have of a soldier in the hospital that day, indicates that a choice of captivity or parole was offered. This "S. B. Johnson" may be Samuel B. Johnson, musician of the 14th Wisconsin Infantry. Of all the S. B. Johnsons listed in the National Park Service's Civil War Soldiers and Sailors database, he is the only S. B. Johnson to have been with a unit that was present at Shiloh. It was well known that the Exchange Hotel hospital was filled with wounded from Shiloh. Also, Wisconsin is specifically named as one of the states possessing wounded in the Exchange Hotel hospital at Newburg in *DEJ*, June 7, 1862. Also see *DEJ*, July 4, 1862. Lieutenant Colonel Hancock of the 14th Wisconsin places a call for all recovered soldiers in Evansville area hospitals to report for duty. A parole of honor in 1862 was an oath not to participate in wartime activities until one was exchanged for a paroled soldier on the other side.

37. *DEJ*, July 25, 1862.

38. In McReynolds's "A Boy's Recollections of the Civil War," the author is confused on two points: the spelling of Knouse's last name and when Henry W. Knouse was killed. McReynolds implies Henry (Canouse) Knouse was killed before the Newburg raid, but his military records state he was killed in action on October 15, 1864.

39. Jackson, 179; Arnett, 45–48; *PR*, 106–107; Badger, 526; Joyce, 127. After the raid, a new arrangement was established for calling out the guard—the church bell on the

First Cumberland Presbyterian Church would sound the alarm. Had this method been established before the raid, the day's outcome could have been different. *PR* (106) also injects some momentary confusion as to whom Johnson was confronting on the riverfront. Johnson makes reference to the fact that "the home guards were forming to attack us, and their colonel, Bethel, was pointed out standing on the bank of the river." To the Newburg townsfolk, "Colonel Bethel" was not Union Bethell but rather his older brother Thomas Bethell, who was a local military hero and who had in the past held that rank in the Indiana Militia. However, it is clear to me that Johnson is talking about the head of the Newburg Home Guard, and that person was Union Bethell. Adam Johnson wasn't particular as to what rank Union Bethell had, as he refers to him as both a colonel and a captain on *PR* 107 in consecutive sentences. He makes the same reference to "Colonel Bethel" on *PR* 109. In all these cases, he is referring to Indiana Home Guard Captain Union Bethell.

40. *DEJ*, July 21, 1862.

41. *DEJ*, July 21, 1862; Terrell, *IWOR*, vol. 1, 183; Jackson, 179–180; Charles Emery Johnson, 95; *Proceedings of the Southwestern Indiana Historical Society*, Evansville, February 28, 1923, Bulletin No. 18, October 1923, Indiana Historical Commission, State House, Indianapolis, Indiana, 29–30. Phil Hicks is not listed on the roster of Johnson's 10th Kentucky Cavalry. Hicks was a young Southern sympathizer along for the ride. The farm of Mrs. F. A. Hicks is shown directly across the road from the Soaper place on the D. J. Lake & Co., *An Illustrated Historical Atlas of Henderson County, Kentucky, 1880*.

42. *DEJ*, July 21, 24, 1862.

43. *DEJ*, July 21, 25, 1862; *Newburgh Register*, July 19, 1862 (modern commemorative edition); Patterson was identified as the raider who looted Bethell's home in *DEJ*, July 25, 1862. Bethell didn't know his name at that time, but he would learn it well later.

44. *DEJ*, July 19, 31, 1862; Jackson, 179; Richard J. Reid, *Newburgh Raid* (Fordsville, Kentucky, 1992), 14–15; Burleigh, 193.

45. *DEJ*, July 4, 19, 1862; *Indiana Magazine of History*, September 1936, vol. 32, 210–216; Snepp, *John W. Foster, Evansville's Distinguished Citizen*, 16; Snepp, "Evansville's Channels of Trade and the Secessionist Movement, 1850–1865," Indiana Historical Society Publications, vol. 8, no. 7, (Indianapolis, 1928), 372; For the Marine Hospital opened in 1856, see Joseph P. Elliott, *A History of Evansville and Vanderburgh County, Indiana* (Evansville, 1897), 223; For the Military Hospital opened in early 1862, see *Indiana in the Civil War* (Indianapolis, 1964), 24; Brant & Fuller, *History of Vanderburgh County, Indiana* (1889), 551; The Jackson, Union, and Evansville Artillery Batteries were involved in responding. Alternate spelling of McFerson may be "McPherson."

46. *NADL*, July 21, 1862; *DEJ*, July 19, 21, 1862; Lemcke, 189–194; *Indiana Magazine of History*, vol. 37, December 1941, 372. Henry Dexter, J. V. Throop, and Gus Dusouchet jointly purchased the *Courier* in 1861 as part of the Paducah & Cairo

Packet Company. Henry Dexter's main boat was the *Charley Bowen*, and coworker Augustus Lemcke's boat was the *Courier*. It is ironic that Dexter commandeers the *Courier* for both his big Independence Day party and for his valiant attempt to stop Adam Johnson's Newburg getaway, even though it is not his regular boat. The *Courier* sinks between Cairo and Mound City, Illinois, on August 22, 1864. For details on the steamer *Commercial,* see Way, boat #1266. The *Commercial* sank at Evansville in 1872.

47. *NADL*, July 21, 1862; *DEJ*, July 19, 21, 1862; *PR*, 107; McReynolds, "A Boy's Recollections of the Civil War"; Charles Emery Johnson, 95.

48. *DEJ*, July 25, 1862; *PR*, 107; D. J. Lake & Co., *An Illustrated Historical Atlas of Henderson County, Kentucky, 1880*, shows a possible route for Martin's escape.

49. *PR*, 107; Starling, 401; Badger, 526.

50. *PR*, 107–108; *DEJ*, July 19, 21, 1862; *NADL*, July 21, 1862; *New York Times*, July 22, 1862; Michael B. Ballard, in "Deceived in Newburgh," *Civil War Times Illustrated*, vol. 21, no. 7, November 1982, 26, states, "Two bluecoats fell, wounded." Ballard's source for this reference appears to be Johnson's official report to General Breckinridge of July 21, 1862; *Indiana Magazine of History*, vol. 37, December 1941, 364, gives a few brief facts about the *Eugene*. For more, see Way, boat #1904. She sank in November 1862, near Fort Pillow, Tennessee.

51. *PR*, 107–108; *DEJ*, July 21, 1862; The *NADL* of July 21, 1862, confirms the general events for Mefford and Carney, but has the victims' names reversed. We know this as Mefford survived the night and Carney did not. Folklore has it that Carney's body was dumped in the Ohio River late that evening and never recovered.

52. *DEJ*, July 21, 1862; *NADL*, July 21, 1862; *Cannelton Reporter* (hereafter referred to as *CR*), July 25, 1862; McReynolds, "A Boy's Recollections of the Civil War."

53. *DEJ*, July 19, 21, 1862.

54. *DEJ*, July 19, 21, 30, 1862.

55. *DEJ*, August 26, 1860, July 21, 25, 1862; Blythe to Morton, July 18, 1862, MTB GD 4; Blythe to Morton, July 19, 1862, MTB GD 4; Morton to Blythe, July 19, 1862, MTB GD 4; Reid, 17; For Coker's occupation and native state, see *Warrick County, Indiana, 1860 Federal Census*; Coker (or Koker), a staunch Democrat, had gotten himself into lasting trouble when he fired a pistol shot into a gathered crowd during a Republican Party rally in Newburg just before the 1860 presidential election, wounding one man in the shoulder. Perhaps the accumulation of politically partisan events just caught up with Coker after the raid; List of those arrested from *DEJ*, July 21, 1862. Hurst, Lee, and Huston were Newburg residents listed as Kentucky natives in census reports; Holloway to Stanton, July 21, 1862, *ORA*, vol. 16, chap. 28, pt. 1, 813–814; For Tilman's background, Crenshaw, et al., 37–38; For Tilman's role in the organization of the Newburg Home Guards see *Our First One Hundred Years*, Newburgh Lodge No. 174, F & A. M., 1955; Terrell, *IWOR*, vol. 1, 184; Colonel

William E. Hollingsworth, commanding the 2nd Regiment of the Indiana Legion, also mounted a rescue mission via the quickest land route but arrived after the *Eugene*.

56. McReynolds, "A Boy's Recollections of the Civil War"; *DEJ*, July 21, 1862; *HWR*, July 24, 1862. Duncan is not named in any newspaper account as the man who shot Mefford, but court documents do name him. Newburg was not in a hurry to try Duncan on the charge, as his arraignment wasn't until March 1868. Duncan's bond was set at $2,000, and a citizens committee was formed to pay it. Among those who signed on for a portion of the bond payment were Union Bethell, Daniel F. Bates, John H. Darby, and J. R. Tilman. The National Park Service's Civil War Soldiers and Sailors System is referenced for Duncan's unit. Duncan had three other family members in the Union army. Copies of the relevant Warrick County, Vanderburgh County, and Gibson County Court records provided by Warrick County historian Kay Lant; Goodspeed Brothers, 68–69, says Ira Duncan was later acquitted on the murder charge.

57. *Indianapolis Daily Journal*, July 19, 1862.

BOOK III
Evansville, Indiana

1. William Foulke, *Life of Oliver P. Morton*, vol. 1, 3–7.

2. Ibid., 6–7.

3. Ibid., 8–10.

4. Ibid., 29–33, 38–39.

5. Ibid., 47–58.

6. Ibid., 101.

7. Ibid., 184; Blythe to Morton, July 18, 1862, MTB GD 4.

8. Morton to Blythe and Blythe to Morton, July 18, 1862, MTB GD 4.

9. Foulke, 184.

10. Boyle to Cairo, July 18, 1862, *Official Records of the Union and Confederate Navies in the War of the Rebellion* (hereafter referred to as *ORN*), series 1, vol. 23, 262; Morton to Pennock, July 18, 1862, MTB GD 4; Morton to Stanton, July 18, 1862, MTB GD 4.

11. Pennock to Davis, July 24, 1862, *ORN*, series 1, vol. 23, 264–265; Strong to Quinby, July 19, 1862, *ORA*, vol. 16, chap. 28, pt. 1, 814; Letter, Yates to Strong, July 14, 1862; Letter, Salomon to Strong, June 27, 1862, Abraham Lincoln Letters, Library of Congress, Washington DC

12. Wise to Foote, July 21, 1862, *ORN*, series 1, vol. 23, 266–268; Pennock to Davis, July 24, 1862, *ORN*, series 1, vol. 23, 264–265.

13. Wise to Foote, July 21, 1862, *ORN*, series 1, vol. 23, 266–268; Terrell, *IWOR*, vol. 1, 188; Pennock to Welles, July 19, 1862, *ORN*, series 1, vol. 23, 263.

14. *DEJ*, July 19, 1862; Blythe to Morton, July 18, 1862, MTB GD 4; Morton to Brooks, July 19, 1862, MTB GD 4. The *Horner*'s intended destination is derived from Governor Morton's request to New Albany post Quartermaster Captain James C. Brooks. There is some confusion about the name of this ship. The *DEJ* continually refers to it as the *Hornet*. Official communication *ORN*, series 1, vol. 23, 532; Chester G. Hearn's *Ellet's Brigade* (Baton Rouge, 2000), 81, and *CR*, July 25, 1862, refer to it as either the *T. D. Horner* or simply the *Horner*. I've used *Horner* throughout. It's possible that the ship's nickname was the *Hornet* or that a mistranscription crept in at some point and stuck.

15. Hearn, 1–42.

16. Eb(h)rman to Strong, July 18, 1862, *ORA*, vol. 16, chap. 28, pt. 1, 815; Blythe to Morton, July 18, 1862, MTB GD 4; Morton to Blythe, July 18, 1862, MTB GD 4; Terrell, *IWOR*, vol. 1, 187.

17. Terrell, *IWOR*, vol. 1, 184; Blythe to Morton, July 18, 19, 1862, MTB GD 4; Kibbey to Morton, July 19, 1862, MTB GD 4; Morton to Kibbey, July 19, 1862, MTB GD 4.

18. *DEJ*, July 24, 26, 1862; *NADL*, July 21, 1862; Terrell, *IWOR*, vol. 1, 186; *Indianapolis Daily Journal*, July 21, 1862; *Indianapolis Sentinel*, July 21, 1862.

19. Topping to Morton, July 19, 1862, MTB GD 4; E. B. Allen in Terre Haute to Morton, July 19, 1862, MTB GD 4; *DEJ*, July 21, 1862; M. D. Topping's successful mission to Henderson would later make him lieutenant colonel of the ill-fated 71st Indiana Infantry Regiment. Topping was killed at the Battle of Richmond, Kentucky, in late August 1862 where the raw recruits of the 71st Indiana were captured whole.

20. E. B. Allen in Terre Haute to Morton, July 19, 1862, MTB GD 4; *DEJ*, July 24, 1862; Terrell, *IWOR*, vol. 1, 187; Morton to E. B. Allen in Terre Haute, July 19, 1862, MTB GD 4.

21. Love to Morton, July 19, 1862, MTB GD 4; Morton to Boyle, July 19, 1862, MTB GD 4; Holloway to Stanton, July 21, 1862, MTB GD 4; Terrell, *IWOR*, vol. 1, 186–188.

22. *DEJ*, July 25, 1862; Terrell, *IWOR*, vol. 1, 187; Hearn, 13.

23. *DEJ*, July 25, 1862. Five miles "below" Spottsville means five miles "downriver" from Spottsville; D. J. Lake & Co.'s, 1880 *An Illustrated Historical Atlas of Henderson County, Kentucky*, shows a path likely used by Martin.

24. *DEJ*, July 21, 23, 24, 25, 1862; *NADL*, July 25, 26, 1862.

25. *CR*, July 25, 1862; *Princeton Clarion*, July 26, 1862.

26. *DEJ*, July 18, 19, 21, 24, 26, 29, 1862.

27. *DEJ*, July 22, 1862.

28. Foulke, 185; *DEJ*, July 22, 23, 1862.

29. "The hospital robber and his 40 thieves" was a stamp used by the *DEJ* almost every day after the raid and became the newspaper's favorite characterization of Johnson and his men. It has some truth to it, as Johnson's men robbed the hospitals in both Henderson and Newburg within a twenty-four hour period; Johnson fondly remembers the moniker as the "River Robber" in *PR*, 121.

30. *DEJ*, July 30, 1862; Terrell, *IWOR*, vol. 1, 188; *Princeton Clarion*, July 26, 1862.

31. Morton to Indianapolis (?), July 22, 1862, MTB GD 4; Pennock to Davis, July 24, 1862, *ORN*, series 1, vol. 23, 264–265; Terrell, *IWOR*, vol. 1, 188–189.

32. *DEJ*, July 23, 30, 1862.

33. *DEJ*, July 23, 25, 30, 1862; Riggs's age, occupation, and native state are from the *Warrick County, Indiana, 1860 Federal Census*; Charles Emery Johnson, 149.

34. *DEJ*, July 30, 1862.

35. *DEJ*, July 23, 1862; J. J. Griffin and a Mr. Wilson from Henderson were arrested as reported in the *HWR*, July 24, 1862; George Smith's diary records the presence of Confederate soldiers in Henderson on July 18, 1862, the day after Johnson's main force left town.

36. *DEJ*, July 23, 1862; *PR*, 106 and the *HWR*, July 24, 1862, state that the soldiers were armed. Dr. Tilman's account in the *DEJ*, July 25, 1862, and the soldiers themselves say they were not. It's likely that the soldiers were in the process of arming themselves when Adam Johnson came in and got the drop on them.

37. *PR*, 109, 110, 345.

38. Johnson to Breckinridge, July 21, 1862, *ORA*, vol. 16, chap. 28, pt. 2, 994–995. Although Johnson has his sequence and dating correct, his figures were all too high. The quantity of cavalry at Henderson and Madisonville, the muskets captured, the prisoners paroled, and the casualties inflicted are all too high when cross-checked against other accounts.

39. *DEJ*, July 24, 26, 1862; Terrell, *IWOR*, vol. 1, 187–189.

40. *DEJ*, July 30, 1862.

41. *DEJ*, July 30, 1862; Starling, 388; Terrell, *IWOR*, vol. 1, 189. The fact that Johnson's memoir makes no mention of the recaptured weapons tells us something about the nature of the information in *Partisan Rangers*. In *PR* (112) Johnson states the weapons were "distributed" but that he needed more shortly. Morton to Boyle, July 24, 1862, MTB GD 4 states, "20 muskets and some pistols" were recovered. Willie Fields was later released and became a member of the Partisan Rangers, Company B.

42. *PR*, 345; *DEJ*, July 30, 1862.

43. *HWR*, July 31, 1862; Starling, 388–390; *Princeton Clarion*, July 26, 1862; *PR*, 110; *DEJ*, July 30, 31, August 1, 1862; Head, 48–49; Joyce, 124–128; Starling names a Dr. McGill as the triggerman for Patterson's wounding. An intriguing possibility is that the man who tried to execute Patterson was Newburg's own Dr. James N. McGill.

44. *PR*, 110, 345–346; Starling, 390.

45. According to *DEJ*, July 26, 1862, the Gavin attack was made on July 24, but the *HWR* of July 31, 1862, says the attack occurred on Friday, July 25; See *PR* between 312 and 313 for a photograph of Lorenzo Fisher.

46. Arnett, 236; *PR*, 110; *DEJ*, July 26, 1862; Starling, 390–391, 395.

47. Starling, 391.

48. *DEJ*, July 26, 1862; Johnson's account of this attack in *PR* (110) is somewhat muddled with the inference that Captain Bethell, whom Johnson calls "Colonel" Bethell, was wounded. It was Colonel James Gavin who was wounded.

49. *DEJ*, July 26, 1862; Starling, 391.

50. Dorris, 74; *HWR*, July 31, 1862.

51. Starling, 391–392; *PR*, 310, says Fisher was killed in 1862, but Starling says he was killed in 1864.

52. *DEJ*, July 25, 1862. The so-called "flags" were probably miniatures sewn onto clothing.

53. *DEJ*, July 30, 1862.

54. *NADL*, July 26, 1862.

55. *DEJ*, July 25, 1862.

56. Morton to Boyle, July 25, 1862; Love to Morton, July 25, 1862; Love to Morton, July 26, 1862, all in MTB GD 4.

57. *DEJ*, July 28, 1862.

58. Ibid.

59. Several examples in *HWR*, July 31, 1862; Starling, 211.

60. *HWR*, July 31, 1862.

61. *HWR*, July 31, 1862; *PR*, 282; Dorris, 37; Felix Eakin, one of the Newburg raiders, was wounded during the West Franklin, Indiana, excursion and soon captured by Federal soldiers.

62. Terrell, *IWOR*, vol. 1, 189; Starling, 211.

63. *DEJ*, July 24, 1862.

64. *New York Times*, November 29, 1862; G. R. Tredway, *Democratic Opposition to the Lincoln Administration in Indiana* (Indianapolis, 1973), 63; *PR*, 235; Reid, 17. Although this comment by Starling refers to Mefford and Carney, it would certainly apply to all others if it applied to them.

65. *PR*, 144–145, 148–150.

66. Tredway, 183–186; *PR*, 173; Beverley Scobell, "The War at Home," *Illinois Issues*, June, 1999; Terrell, *IWOR*, vol. 1, 262–266 for General Hovey's raid on Johnson's men.

Bibliography

Adams, Edwin. *History of Warrick County, Indiana*. Evansville, Indiana: Crescent City, 1868.

Armstrong, J. M. *Biographical Encyclopaedia of Kentucky of the Dead and Living Men of the Nineteenth Century*. Cincinnati: 1878 (copy resides in the Henderson County Public Library).

Arnett, Maralea. *The Annals & Scandals of Henderson County, Kentucky 1775–1975*. Corydon, Kentucky: Fremar Publishing Company, 1976.

Ballard, Michael B. "Deceived in Newburgh: To Capture an Arsenal." *Civil War Times Illustrated*, November 1982, 23–26.

Bentley Historical Library, University of Michigan.

John Sidney Andrews Papers, consisting of:

Letters of Luther F. Hale to John Sidney Andrews, July 8, 10, 11, 1862

Letter of George B. Tyler to John Sidney Andrews, date unknown

Bethell, Union Noble. Bethell family tree compilation. Unpublished, 1932 (copy resides with Kay Lant).

Bethell–Warren Papers, William Henry Smith Memorial Library, Indiana Historical Society, Indianapolis, Indiana.

Bigham, Darrel E. *Towns and Villages of the Lower Ohio*. Lexington, Kentucky: University Press of Kentucky, 1998.

A Biographical History of Eminent and Self-Made Men of the State of Indiana. Cincinnati, Ohio: Western Biographical Publishing Company, 1880 (copy resides in the Evansville–Vanderburgh Central Library).

Black, Glen. "Angel and Carney Family Tree." 1959 (copy resides with Don Claspell).

Brant & Fuller. *History of Vanderburgh County, Indiana*. Evansville, Indiana: 1889 (resides in the Newburgh Public Library).

Briggs, Richard A. *The Saga of Fort Duffield: Kentucky's Civil War Treasure*. West Point, Kentucky: Friends of Fort Duffield, 1999.

Browning, Charles. "People Study Notecard for Henry T. Dexter." Photocopy, Evansville–Vanderburgh Public Library, Evansville, Indiana.

Burleigh, William, ed. *A Bicentennial Look at Newburgh, Indiana, 1776–1976*. Newburgh, Indiana: Newburgh Public Library, 1976.

Captain Jacob Warrick Chapter of the National Association of the Daughters of the American Revolution, Boonville, Indiana. *Warrick County, Indiana, 1860 Federal Census*. Owensboro, Kentucky: Cook-McDowell Publications, 1981.

Claspell, Donald. "Angel-Carney Family Tree." 1996 (copy resides with Don Claspell).

Collins, Lewis, and Richard H. Collins. *History of Kentucky*. Vol. 1. Covington, Kentucky: 1882 (copy resides in the Henderson County Public Library).

Connelly, Thomas Lawrence. *Army of the Heartland, The Army of Tennessee, 1861–1862*. Baton Rouge, Louisiana: Louisiana State University Press, 1967.

Coons, John W., comp. *Indiana at Shiloh*. Indianapolis, Indiana: Indiana Shiloh National Park Service Commission, 1904 (copy resides in the Willard Library, Evansville, Indiana).

Cramer, Zadok. *The Navigator*. Pittsburgh, Pennsylvania: Cramer & Spear, 1811.

Crenshaw, Jane; B. Parker, M. Forsythe, and M. Tromly, (Historical Marker Book Committee). *Historical Markers Erected by the Women's Club of Newburgh, Indiana, 1975–1979*. Newburgh, Indiana (copy resides in the Newburgh Public Library).

Cumings, Samuel. *The Western Pilot; Containing Charts of the Ohio River and of the Mississippi*. Cincinnati, Ohio: George Conclin, 1847.

Cunningham, S. A., ed. *Confederate Veteran Magazine*, Vol. 6, March 1898; Vol. 8, December 1900; Vol. 12, December 1904; Vol. 23, July 1915. Hardbound reprint of the twelve issues for each year. Wendell, North Carolina: Broadfoot's Bookmark.

Dannheiser, Freda Jacobs, comp. *Henderson County, Kentucky, Census Records for 1860*. Henderson, Kentucky: 1969.

Davis, William J., ed. *Partisan Rangers of the Confederate States Army, Memoirs of Adam R. Johnson*. Austin, Texas: State House Press, 1995 (reprint of the Louisville, 1904 original published by George G. Fetter & Company).

Degregorio, William A. *The Complete Book of U.S. Presidents, Third Edition*. New York, New York: Grammercy Books, 1991.

The Department of History of Indiana University in Cooperation with the Indiana Historical Society, Bloomington, Indiana, *Indiana Magazine of History*. September 1935; September 1936; December 1941; June 1944; June 1945.

Devine, Michael J. *John W. Foster: Politics and Diplomacy in the Imperial Era, 1873–1917*. Athens, Ohio: Ohio University Press, 1981.

Dictionary of American Naval Fighting Ships. Vol. 1B. Washington, D.C.: Department of the Navy, U.S. Naval Historical Center, 1959.

Dorris, Mendy. *Tug of War, The Civil War in Henderson County, Kentucky*. Henderson, Kentucky: 1996 (copy resides with the Henderson County Historical and Genealogical Society).

Dorris, Mendy & L. Hallmark, comps. *Henderson County, Kentucky: The Civil War Walking and/or Driving Tour*. Henderson, Kentucky: 1998 (copy resides in the Henderson County Historical and Genealogical Society).

Duke, Basil. *A History of Morgan's Cavalry*. Bloomington, Indiana: Indiana University Press, 1960.

Eisenhower, John S. D. *So Far From God; The U.S. War with Mexico 1846–1848.* New York, New York: Doubleday, 1989.

Elliott, Joseph P. *A History of Evansville and Vanderburgh County, Indiana.* Evansville, Indiana: Keller Printing Company, 1897.

Esarey, Logan. *History of Indiana From Its Exploration to 1922.* Vol. 2. Dayton, Ohio: Dayton Historical Society Publishing Company, 1922.

Eva M. Bethell. "Remarks at her funeral." Photocopy, Newburgh Public Library.

Feigel, Barbara Anne. "Civil War in the Western Ohio Valley as Viewed From Evansville, Indiana" (master's thesis, Indiana University, 1957).

Fortune, Will, ed. *Warrick and Its Prominent People.* Evansville, Indiana: Courier Company, 1881 (copy resides with the Newburgh Public Library).

Foulke, William D. *The Life of Oliver P. Morton.* 2 vols. The Bowen–Merrill Company, Indianapolis, 1899.

Garde, Carol & James Garde. *The Early Bethells and Their Descendants 1635–1994.* Interlaken, New York: Heart of the Lakes Publishing, 1994.

Goodrich, Thomas. *Black Flag, Guerrilla Warfare on the Western Border, 1861–1865.* Bloomington, Indiana: Indiana University Press, 1995.

Goodspeed Brothers. *History of Warrick, Spencer, and Perry Counties.* Chicago, Illinois: 1885 (copy resides with the Evansville–Vanderburgh Central Library).

Greene, W. P. *The Green River Country from Bowling Green to Evansville—Its Traffic, Its Resources, Its Towns and Its People.* Evansville, Indiana: J. S. Reilly, 1898.

Griffing, B. N. *An Illustrated Historical Atlas of Warrick County, Indiana.* Philadelphia, Pennyslvania: D. J. Lake & Co., 1880.

Griffing, B. N. *Griffing's Atlas of Vanderburgh County, Indiana.* Philadelphia, Pennyslvania: 1880.

Hammond, Debbie, trans. *1860 Federal Census of Hopkins County.* Kentucky: Hopkins County Genealogical Society.

Harralson, Agnes S. *Steamboats on the Green and the Colorful Men Who Operated Them.* Berea, Kentucky: Kentucke Imprints, 1981.

Harrison, Lowell H. *The Civil War in Kentucky.* Louisville, Kentucky: University Press of Kentucky, 1975.

Head, James Louis. *The Atonement of John Brooks.* Geneva, Florida: Heritage Press, 2001.

Hearn, Chester G. *Ellet's Brigade, The Strangest Outfit of All.* Baton Rouge, Louisiana: Louisiana State University Press, 2000.

Henderson County Genealogical Society. *175th Anniversary of Kentucky Historical and Biographical Notes.* Henderson, Kentucky, 1967.

Illustrated Historical Atlas of the State of Indiana. Chicago, Illinois: Baskin, Forster & Co., 1876.

Indiana in the Civil War, Indianapolis, Indiana: Indiana Civil War Centennial Commission, 1964.

Indiana in the War of the Rebellion, Report of the Adjutant General of the State of Indiana. Indianapolis, 1869.

Inventory of the County Archives of Indiana, No. 87 Warrick County (Boonville). Indianapolis, Indiana: The Indiana Historical Records Survey, 1940.

Jackson, Adah, ed. "Glimpses of Civil War Newburg, An Account of Eliza Bethell Warren's Girlhood in Newburg, Indiana, 1855–1870." *Indiana Magazine of History.* Vol. 41. June 1945.

Johnson, Charles Emery. *One Hundred Years of Evansville, Indiana, 1812–1912 with Miscellanea.* Evansville, Indiana: 1948 (copy resides in the Bower–Suhrheinrich Library at the University of Evansville, Indiana).

Johnson, E. Polk. *History of Kentucky and Kentuckians.* Vol. 2. Chicago, Illinois: The Lewis Publishing Company, 1912.

Johnson, Michael L. "Civil War Military History of Warrick County, Indiana." (Date not given. Typed manuscript provided by Kay Lant.)

Joyce, Fred. "Why Sue Mundy Became a Guerrilla." *Southern Bivouac*, Vol. 2, November 1883. Reprinted by Broadfoot Publishing Company, Wilmington, North Carolina, 1992.

King, Gail & Susan Thurman. *Currents—Henderson's River Book.* Henderson, Kentucky: Henderson County Public Library, 1991 (copy resides in Henderson County Public Library).

Kleber, John E., ed. *The Kentucky Encyclopedia.* Lexington, Kentucky: University Press of Kentucky, 1992.

Klein, Benjamin. *The Ohio River Handbook and Picture Album.* Cincinnati, Ohio: Young and Klein, Inc., 1969.

Lake, D. J. & Co. and B. N. Griffing. *An Illustrated Historical Atlas of Henderson County, Kentucky.* Evansville, Indiana: Unigraphic, 1880.

Lake, D. J. & Co. and B. N. Griffing. *An Illustrated Historical Atlas of Henderson and Union Counties, Kentucky.* Evansville, Indiana: Unigraphic, 1880.

Leary, Ethel C. *Who's Who on the Ohio River and Its Tributaries, An Ohio River Anthology.* Cincinnati, Ohio: Ethel C. Leary Publishing Co., 1931.

Lemcke, Augustus J. *Reminiscences of an Indianian.* Indianapolis, Indiana: The Hollenback Press, 1905.

Lewis, Gerald R. and the Newburgh School History Book '96 Committee. *Newburgh, Indiana; A History of Schools and Families, 1803–1959.* Mt. Vernon, Indiana: Windmill Publications, 1996.

Library of Congress, Washington DC

    Abraham Lincoln Papers consisting of:

        Letter, Richard Yates to General William K. Strong, July 14, 1862

        Letter, Edward Salomon to General William K. Strong, June 27, 1862

Lloyd's Official Map of Kentucky, 1863. New York, New York: J. T. Lloyd, 1863.

Love, John. Papers at the William Henry Smith Memorial Library, Indiana Historical Society, Indianapolis.

Lynn, Stephen. Condensed History of the 10th (Johnson's) Kentucky Cavalry, C.S.A. 2000. ftp://ftp.rootsweb.com/pub/usgenweb/ky/military/rosters/conf/10kycav.txt (accessed 2003).

Map of Precinct Number 21, Mill District in Magisterial District Number 7, Atlanta, Georgia: W. G. Fish Publishing, 1898.

McReynolds, Robert. "A Boy's Recollections of the Civil War." *The Colorado Springs Evening Sun*, 1905. Taken from a typed, undated manuscript provided by Kay Lant.

Memoirs of the Lower Ohio Valley. 2 vols. Madison, Wisconsin: Federal Publishing Company, 1905.

Miller, Milford M. *The Evansville Fleet During the Civil War.* Evansville, Indiana. Typed manuscript at the Willard Library, Evansville, Indiana.

Monaghan, Jay. *Civil War on the Western Border, 1854–1865.* Toronto, Canada: Little, Brown and Company, Toronto, 1955.

Morrison, Olin Lee. *Indiana at Civil War Time, A Contribution to the Centennial Publications.* Athens, Ohio: EM Morrison, 1961.

National Archives, Washington DC "John Hathaway Darby War Department Archive."

The Newburgh, Indiana, Sesquicentennial, 1803–1953 (pamphlet, resides in the Newburgh, Indiana, Public Library).

Newspapers
    Boonville Enquirer
    Cannelton Reporter
    Daily Evansville Journal
    Evansville Courier-Press
    Evansville Press
    Henderson Weekly Reporter
    Indianapolis Daily Journal
    Indianapolis Sentinel
    London Times
    New Albany Daily Ledger
    Newburgh Register
    New York Times
    Princeton Clarion

Official Records of the Union and Confederate Navies in the War of the Rebellion, 1894–1922.

Governor Oliver P. Morton Telegram Book, General Dispatches No. 4, 6–11–62 to 7–31–62. Indiana State Archives, Commission on Public Records, Indianapolis.

Our First One Hundred Years, Newburgh Lodge No. 174, F & A. M. (booklet). Newburgh, Indiana, 1955 (copy resides with Kay Lant).

Phillips, Oscar J., & Phillips, Opal B., comp. *Warrick County, Indiana, 1850 Census*. Owensboro, Kentucky: McDowell Publications, 1980.

Proceedings of the Southwestern Indiana Historical Society, Evansville, Indiana, February 28, 1923, Bulletin No. 18, October, 1923. Indiana Historical Commission, State House, Indianapolis (copy resides with Kay Lant).

Ramage, James A. *Rebel Raider, The Life of John Hunt Morgan*. Lexington, Kentucky: The University Press of Kentucky, 1986.

Reid, Richard J. *Newburgh Raid, Featuring a Biographical Sketch of Brig. General Adam R. Johnson*. Fordsville, Kentucky: Sandefur Printing, 1992.

Report of the Adjutant General of the State of Kentucky, Confederate Kentucky Volunteers, War of 1861–1865. Vol. 2. Printed by authority of the Legislature of Kentucky, 1918 (reprinted by Cook-McDowell Publications, 1980).

Rowell, John W. *Yankee Cavalrymen; Through the Civil War with the Ninth Pennsylvania Cavalry*. Knoxville, Tennessee: University of Tennessee Press, 1971.

Scobell, Beverley. "The War at Home." *Illinois Issues*, June 1999.

Smith, Barbara, comp. *Warrick County, Indiana, 1850 Census*. Owensboro, Kentucky: Genealogical Reference Company, 1980.

Smith, George. Transcription of personal diary, 1859–1873 (copy resides in the Henderson County, Kentucky, Library).

Snepp, Daniel W. "Evansville's Channels of Trade and the Secessionist Movement, 1850–1865." *Indiana Historical Society Publications*, Vol. 8, No. 7, 1928.

Snepp, Daniel W. *John W. Foster, Evansville's Distinguished Citizen*. Evansville, Indiana: 1975.

Snepp, Daniel W. "John W. Foster: Diplomat and Statesman" (doctoral thesis at Indiana University, 1934). Photocopy, Evansville–Vanderburgh Central Library, Evansville, Indiana.

Snepp, Daniel W. *Sidelights of Early Evansville History*. Evansville, Indiana: 1974.

Snepp, Daniel W. *Sidelights of Early Evansville History, Revised Edition*. Evansville, Indiana: 1976.

Soldier of Indiana in the War for the Union. Indianapolis, Indiana: Merrill and Co., 1866 (copy resides at the Willard Library, Evansville, Indiana).

Starling, Edmund L. *History of Henderson County, Kentucky*. 1887. Reprinted in 1972 by Unigraphic, Inc., Evansville, Indiana.

Swiggett, Howard. *The Rebel Raider, A Life of John Hunt Morgan*. Garden City, New York: The Garden City Publishing Co., 1937.

Sword, Wiley. *Shiloh: Bloody April*. Dayton, Ohio: Press of the Morningside Bookshop, 2001.

Terrell, W. H. H. *Report of the Adjutant General of the State of Indiana, 1861–1865*. Vols. 1–8. Indianapolis, Indiana: Samuel M. Douglass, State Printer, 1866. Reprinted by the Indiana Historical Society, Indianapolis, 1960.

Thomas, Edison H. *John Hunt Morgan and His Raiders*. Lexington, Kentucky: The University Press of Kentucky, 1975.

Thornbrough, Emma Lou. *Indiana in the Civil War Era, 1850–1880*. Indianapolis, Indiana: Indiana Historical Bureau & Indiana Historical Society, 1965.

Thornbrough, Gayle and Paula Corpuz, eds. *The Diary of Calvin Fletcher, Volume VII, Including Letters to and from Calvin Fletcher*. Indianapolis, Indiana: Indiana Historical Society, 1980.

Tredway, G. R. *Democratic Opposition to the Lincoln Administration in Indiana*. Indianapolis, Indiana: Indiana Historical Bureau, 1973.

University of Notre Dame, Thomas Family Correspondence, Manuscripts from the American Civil War, University of Notre Dame, Department of Rare Books and Special Collections in the Hesburgh Library. Letter of George Thomas to Minerva Thomas, July 24, 1862.

The War of the Rebellion: A Compilation of the Official Records of the Union and Confederate Armies, 1880–1901.

Watson, Thomas Shelby. *The Silent Riders*. Louisville, Kentucky: Beechmont Press, 1971.

Way, Frederick, Jr. *Way's Packet Directory, 1848–1994, Revised Edition*. Athens, Ohio: Ohio University Press, 1994.

White, Edward, ed. *Evansville and Its Men of Mark*. Evansville, Indiana: Historical Publishing Company, 1873.

Winslow, Hattie Lou & Joseph R. H. Moore. *Camp Morton 1861–1865*. Indianapolis, Indiana: Indiana Historical Society, 1995.

Wood, W. J. *Battles of the Revolutionary War, 1775–1781*. Chapel Hill, North Carolina: Algonquin Books of Chapel Hill, 1990.

Wooden, Howard E. *Architectural Heritage of Evansville, An Interpretive Review of the 19th Century*. Evansville, Indiana: Evansville Museum of Arts and Science, 1962.

978-0-595-83623-9
0-595-83623-2

CPSIA information can be obtained
at www.ICGtesting.com
Printed in the USA
LVHW091423080419
613372LV00013B/573/P